A GOLDEN TREASURY
OF IRISH VERSE

Complete & Unabridged

More poetry available from
Macmillan Collector's Library

Poems About Birds ed. H. J. Massingham
Sunrise ed. Susie Gibbs
Happy Hour: Poems to Raise a Glass to
introduced by Jancis Robinson
Poems for Stillness introduced by Ana Sampson
Poems of the Sea introduced by Adam Nicolson
Poems for Happiness introduced by Richard Coles
Poems for Travellers introduced by Paul Theroux
Poems for Christmas introduced by Judith Flanders
Poems of Childhood introduced by Michael
Morpurgo
Poems on Nature introduced by Helen Macdonald
Poems for Love introduced by Joanna Trollope
Poems for New Parents ed. Becky Brown
The Golden Treasury ed. Francis Turner Palgrave
Poetry of the First World War ed. Marcus Clapham

COLLECTIONS

Goblin Market & Other Poems by Christina Rossetti
Leaves of Grass: Selected Poems by Walt Whitman
Selected Poems by John Keats
Poems of Thomas Hardy by Thomas Hardy
Collected Poems by W. B. Yeats
The Sonnets by William Shakespeare
Tales and Poems by Edgar Allan Poe
A Shropshire Lad by A. E. Housman
The Rime of the Ancient Mariner
by Samuel Taylor Coleridge

A GOLDEN TREASURY
OF IRISH VERSE

Edited by
LENNOX ROBINSON

MACMILLAN COLLECTOR'S LIBRARY

First published 1925 by Macmillan & Co.

This edition published 2024 by Macmillan Collector's Library
an imprint of Pan Macmillan
The Smithson, 6 Briset Street, London EC1M 5NR
EU representative: Macmillan Publishers Ireland Ltd,
1st Floor, The Liffey Trust Centre, 117–126 Sheriff Street Upper,
Dublin 1, D01 YC43
Associated companies throughout the world
www.panmacmillan.com

ISBN 978-1-0350-2657-9

Poetry selection and foreword copyright © The Abbey Theatre

1 3 5 7 9 8 6 4 2

A CIP catalogue record for this book is available from the British Library.

Cover and endpaper design: Ami Smithson, Pan Macmillan Art Department
Typeset in Plantin by Jouve (UK), Milton Keynes
Printed and bound in China by Imago

Visit **www.panmacmillan.com** to read more
about all our books and to buy them.

Contents

To M.

Foreword

An anthology of poems is the only kind of book for which no apology need ever be offered. I have collected here what seem to me to be some of our most beautiful Irish poems, I have chosen many poems which were originally written in Gaelic and which have been translated by poets into beautiful English, and, unlike many other Irish anthologies, I have included no poem merely because its patriotic sentiments have made it popular.

The book is not arranged chronologically; such an arrangement is of small interest in an Irish anthology where so little of value was written in English before the nineteenth century, nor is it arranged in clearly defined sections of subjects. It follows instead a progression which is, perhaps, clear only to the compiler, but which he hopes means that wherever the book is opened some connection of thought or mood will be found to link poem to succeeding poem.

I must thank "A. E." and Mr. W. B. Yeats for the help they have given me. The book, indeed, owes its existence to "A. E.", and he has been tireless in his interest and help. Neither he nor Mr. Yeats has always agreed with me, but did any anthology satisfy any one except the compiler? It will not satisfy even me by the time these words are printed. And of the many others who have helped me I thank particularly Mr. J. J. O'Neill, Librarian of University College, Dublin, and Mr. Geoffrey Phibbs.

LENNOX ROBINSON

FOXROCK, *Easter* 1924

Acknowledgements

I must gratefully acknowledge the kindness of authors (or their executors) and of publishers in granting me permission to include in this anthology work which is still copyright. I name them here: "A. E."; Mrs. Allingham and Messrs. Longmans, Green & Co., for the poems of William Allingham; "An Pilibin" and the Talbot Press, Ltd.; Mr. Joseph Campbell; Mr. Francis Carlin; Miss E. Chadwick and Mr. Elliot Stock, for Dr. Ghadwick's poem; Mr. Austin Clarke, for extracts from "The Vengeance of Fionn" and from "The Sword of the West"; Mr. Padraic Colum and, in the case of five of his poems, Messrs. Maunsel & Roberts, Ltd.; Messrs. Burns, Oates & Washbourne, Ltd., for the poems by Aubrey de Vere; Mr. E. R. Dodds; Mrs. Dowden and Messrs. J. M. Dent & Sons, for the poems by Professor Edward Dowden; Mr. W. K. Magee, for the poem by "John Eglinton"; Mr. H. S. H. Guinness, for the poems by Sir Samuel Ferguson; Mr. Cecil French; Dr. Oliver Gogarty and the Cuala Press; Captain Stephen

Gwynn and Messrs. Wm. Blackwood & Sons; Mr. John Lane, the Bodley Head, Ltd., for the poems from "Ballads in Prose", by Nora Hopper; Mr. W. Alexander Ingram, for his father's ballad; Messrs. Elkin Mathews, Ltd., for Lionel Johnson's poems; Mr. James Joyce and Messrs. Jonathan Cape, Ltd.; the Educational Company of Ireland, Ltd., for the poem by Robert Dwyer Joyce; Mr. Patrick Kelly; the Talbot Press, Ltd., for T. M. Kettle's poem; Mrs. Helen Donovan (Miss Helen Lanyon); Mr. J. C. Larminie, for his brother's poem; the Hon. Frederick Lawless, for the Hon. Emily Lawless's poems; the Lord Dunsany and Messrs. Herbert Jenkins, Ltd., for the poems by Francis Ledwidge; Mr. Philip Francis Little and Messrs. John Long, Ltd.; Miss Alice Milligan; Miss Susan L. Mitchell and Messrs. Maunsel & Roberts, Ltd.; "A Bud in the Frost" is included by permission of Miss Moira O'Neill, and taken from "More Songs of the Glens of Antrim," and acknowledgement is also due to Messrs. Wm. Blackwood & Sons; Miss Mary Boyle O'Reilly and Mrs. W. E. Hocking, for the poem by their father, John Boyle O'Reilly; Mr. John Lane, the Bodley Head, Ltd., for the poems by Arthur O'Shaughnessy; Mr. Seumas O'Sullivan; Mrs. O. Parnell, for the poem by Fanny Parnell; Mr. Forrest Reid and the Talbot Press, Ltd.; Mrs. T. W. Rolleston, for her husband's poems; Mr. C. K. Shorter and Messrs. Constable & Co., Ltd., for the poems by Dora Sigerson Shorter; Mr. James Stephens; Mr. L. A. G. Strong; Mr. H. Stuart; Messrs. Maunsel & Roberts, Ltd., for the poems by J. M. Synge; the Talbot Press, Ltd., for the poems by John Todhunter; Mr. Harold Williams, for the poems by Herbert Trench; Mrs. Katharine Tynan Hinkson and, in the case of five of her poems from "The Flower of Peace", Messrs. Burns, Oates & Washbourne, Ltd.; Messrs. T. Fisher Unwin, Ltd., for the poems by Mr. Charles Weekes; Messrs. Methuen & Co., Ltd., for three poems by Oscar Wilde from "Charmides," and for an extract from "The Ballad of Reading Gaol," taken from the volume "Selected Poems"; Mr. R. N. D. Wilson; Messrs. T. Fisher Unwin, Ltd., and the author, for four poems by Mr. W. B. Yeats, and the author and Messrs. Macmillan & Co., Ltd., for the remaining ones. In the case of translations from the Gaelic I am also indebted to Mr. R. J. Collender for the poem by Michael Cavanagh; to Mr. Robin Flower; to Lady Gregory; to Miss Eleanor Hull and Messrs. Chatto & Windus, Ltd.; to Dr. Douglas Hyde; to the Talbot

Press, Ltd., for the poem by Thomas MacDonagh; to Miss Antonie Meyer and Messrs. Constable & Co., Ltd., for the poems by Kuno Meyer; to Messrs. T. Fisher Unwin, Ltd., for "Love's Despair," taken from "Bards of the Gael and Gaul," by Dr. George Sigerson. In four cases it has been found impossible to trace the author or his executors, and to them I apologise for my seeming discourtesy. To Messrs. Macmillan & Co. my thanks are especially due, not only for the ready permission they have given in the case of the many poems published by them, but for their tireless care in seeking out the owners of the other copyright poems.

L. R.

An Apology to the Harp

Harp of the land I love! forgive this hand
  That reverently lifts thee from the dust,
And scans thy strings with filial awe and love,
  Lest by neglect the chords of song should rust.

Deep buried in tall grave-yard grass thou wert—
  The shadows to the dead thy sole defence—
The wild flowers twining round thee meekly fond,
  Fearing their very love might be offence.

Seeing thee thus, I knew the bards were gone
  Who thrilled thee—and themselves thrilled to
    thy touch:
Mangan and Moore, I knew, were vanishèd;
  I knelt and raised thee: did I dare too much?

Forgive me! oh, forgive me, if too bold!
  I twine thy chords about my very heart,
And make with every pulse of life a vow,
  Swearing—nor years, nor death, shall us two part.

I have no hope to gather bays, on high
  Beneath the snows of ages, where they bloom,
As many votaries of thine desired,
  And the great favoured few have haply done;

But if an emblem o'er my dust should rise,
    Let it be this: Our Harp within a wreath
Of shamrocks twining round it lovingly,
    That so, O Harp! our love shall know no death!

Thomas D'Arcy McGee

II
The Fair Hills of Ireland

A plenteous place is Ireland for hospitable cheer,
    Uileacan dubh O!
Where the wholesome fruit is bursting from the
    yellow barley ear;
    Uileacan dubh O!
There is honey in the trees where her misty vales
    expand,
And her forest paths, in summer, are by falling
    waters fann'd,
There is dew at high noontide there, and springs i'
    the yellow sand,
        On the fair hills of holy Ireland.

Curl'd he is and ringletted, and plaited to the
    knee,
    Uileacan dubh O!

Each captain who comes sailing across the Irish sea;
  Uileacan dubh O!
And I will make my journey, if life and health but
  stand,
Unto that pleasant country, that fresh and fragrant
  strand,
And leave your boasted braveries, your wealth and
  high command,
  For the fair hills of holy Ireland.

Large and profitable are the stacks upon the
  ground,
  Uileacan dubh O!
The butter and the cream do wondrously abound,
  Uileacan dubh O!
The cresses on the water and the sorrels are at
  hand,
And the cuckoo's calling daily his note of mimic
  bland,
And the bold thrush sings so bravely his song i'
  the forests grand,
  On the fair hills of holy Ireland.

Sir Samuel Ferguson
(From the Irish)

A Day in Ireland

Four sharp scythes sweeping—in concert keeping
   The rich-robed meadow's broad bosom o'er,
Four strong men mowing, with bright health
     glowing,
   A long green sward spread each man before;

With sinews springing—my keen blade swinging,—
   I strode—the fourth man in that blithe band;
As stalk of corn that summer morn,
   The scythe felt light in my stalwart hand.

Oh, King of Glory! How changed my story
   Since in youth's noontide—long, long ago,
I mowed that meadow—no cloudy shadow
   Between my brow and the hot sun's glow;
Fair girls raking the hay—and making
   The fields resound with their laugh and glee,
Their voices ringing—than cuckoo's singing,
   Made music sweeter by far to me.

Bees hovered over the honied clover,
   Then nestward hied upon wings of light;
No use in trying to trace them flying—
   One brief low hum and they're out of sight.

On downy thistle bright insects nestle,
  Or flutter skyward on painted wings,
At times alighting on flowers inviting—
  'Twas pleasant watching the airy things.

From hazel bushes came songs of thrushes
  And blackbirds—sweeter than harper's lay;
While high in ether—with sun-tipped feather—
  The skylark warbled his anthem gay;
With throats distended, sweet linnets blended
  A thousand notes in one glorious chime,
Oh, King Eternal, 'twas life supernal
  In beauteous Erin, that pleasant time.

Michael Cavanagh
(From the Irish)

IV

Ireland

'Twas the dream of a God,
    And the mould of His hand,
That you shook 'neath His stroke,
That you trembled and broke
    To this beautiful land.

Here He loosed from His hold
    A brown tumult of wings,

5

Till the wind on the sea
Bore the strange melody
    Of an island that sings.

He made you all fair,
    You in purple and gold,
You in silver and green,
Till no eye that has seen
    Without love can behold

I have left you behind
    In the path of the past,
With the white breath of flowers,
With the best of God's hours,
    I have left you at last.

Dora Sigerson Shorter

v

Red Hanrahan's Song About Ireland

The old brown thorn trees break in two high over
    Cummen Strand,
Under a bitter black wind that blows from the left
    hand;
Our courage breaks like an old tree in a black
    wind and dies,

But we have hidden in our hearts the flame out of
    the eyes
Of Cathleen, the daughter of Houlihan.

The wind has bundled up the clouds high over
    Knocknarea,
And thrown the thunder on the stones for all that
    Maeve can say.
Angers that are like noisy clouds have set our
    hearts abeat;
But we have all bent low and low and kissed the
    quiet feet
Of Cathleen, the daughter of Houlihan.

The yellow pool has overflowed high up on
    Clooth-na-Bare,
For the wet winds are blowing out of the
    clinging air;
Like heavy flooded waters our bodies and our
    blood;
But purer than a tall candle before the Holy Rood
Is Cathleen, the daughter of Houlihan.

W. B. Yeats

After Aughrim

She said, "They gave me of their best,
They lived, they gave their lives for me;
I tossed them to the howling waste,
And flung them to the foaming sea."

She said, "I never gave them aught,
Not mine the power, if mine the will;
I let them starve, I let them bleed,—
They bled and starved, and loved me still."

She said, "Ten times they fought for me,
Ten times they strove with might and main,
Ten times I saw them beaten down,
Ten times they rose, and fought again."

She said, "I stayed alone at home,
A dreary woman, grey and cold;
I never asked them how they fared,
Yet still they loved me as of old."

She said, "I never called them sons,
I almost ceased to breathe their name,
Then caught it echoing down the wind,
Blown backwards from the lips of Fame."

She said, "Not mine, not mine that fame;
Far over sea, far over land,
Cast forth like rubbish from my shores,
They won it yonder, sword in hand."

She said, "God knows they owe me nought,
I tossed them to the foaming sea,
I tossed them to the howling waste,
Yet still their love comes home to me."

Hon. Emily Lawless

VII

Ways of War

A terrible and splendid trust
Heartens the host of Inisfail:
Their dream is of the swift sword-thrust,
A lightning glory of the Gael.

Croagh Patrick is the place of prayers,
And Tara the assembling place:
But each sweet wind of Ireland bears
The trump of battle on its race.

From Dursey Isle to Donegal,
From Howth to Achill, the glad noise

Rings: and the heirs of glory fall,
Or victory crowns their fighting joys.

A dream! a dream! an ancient dream!
Yet, ere peace come to Inisfail,
Some weapons on some field must gleam,
Some burning glory fire the Gael.

That field may lie beneath the sun
Fair for the treading of an host:
That field in realms of thought be won,
And armed minds do their uttermost:

Some way, to faithful Inisfail,
Shall come the majesty and awe
Of martial truth, that must prevail
To lay on all the eternal law.

Lionel Johnson

VIII

The Nameless Doon

Who were the builders? Question not the silence
That settles on the lake for evermore,
Save when the sea-bird screams and to the islands
The echo answers from the steep-cliffed shore.

O half-remaining ruin, in the lore
Of human life a gap shall all deplore
Beholding thee; since thou art like the dead
Found slain, no token to reveal the why,
The name, the story. Some one murderèd
We know, we guess; and gazing upon thee,
And, filled by thy long silence of reply,
We guess some garnered sheaf of tragedy;—
Of tribe or nation slain so utterly
That even their ghosts are dead, and on their grave
Springeth no bloom of legend in its wildness;
And age by age weak washing round the islands
No faintest sigh of story lisps the wave.

William Larminie

IX

Clonmacnoise

In a quiet water'd land, a land of roses,
     Stands Saint Kieran's city fair;
And the warriors of Erin in their famous
     generations
     Slumber there.

There beneath the dewy hillside sleep the noblest
     Of the clan of Conn,

Each below his stone with name in branching
      Ogham
    And the sacred knot thereon.

There they laid to rest the seven Kings of Tara,
      There the sons of Cairbrè sleep—
Battle-banners of the Gael that in Kieran's plain
      of crosses
    Now their final hosting keep.

And in Clonmacnoise they laid the men of Teffia,
      And right many a lord of Breagh;
Deep the sod above Clan Creidè and Clan Conaill,
      Kind in hall and fierce in fray.

Many and many a son of Conn the
      Hundred-fighter
      In the red earth lies at rest;
Many a blue eye of Clan Colman the turf covers,
      Many a swan-white breast.

T. W. Rolleston
(From the Irish of Angus O'Gillan)

The Fort of Rathangan

The fort over against the oak-wood,
Once it was Bruidge's, it was Cathal's,
It was Aed's, it was Ailill's,
It was Conaing's, it was Cuiline's,
And it was Maeldúin's;
The fort remains after each in his turn—
And the kings asleep in the ground.

Kuno Meyer
(From the Irish)

The Grave of Rury

Clear as air, the western waters
Evermore their sweet, unchanging song
Murmur in their stony channels
Round O'Conor's sepulchre in Cong.

Crownless, hopeless, here he lingered;
Year on year went by him like a dream,
While the far-off roar of conquest
Murmured faintly like the singing stream.

Here he died, and here they tombed him,
Men of Fechin, chanting round his grave.
Did they know, ah! did they know it,
What they buried by the babbling wave?

Now above the sleep of Rury
Holy things and great have passed away;
Stone by stone the stately Abbey
Falls and fades in passionless decay.

Darkly grows the quiet ivy,
Pale the broken arches glimmer through;
Dark upon the cloister-garden
Dreams the shadow of the ancient yew.

Through the roofless aisles the verdure
Flows, the meadow-sweet and fox-glove bloom.
Earth, the mother and consoler,
Winds soft arms about the lonely tomb.

Peace and holy gloom possess him,
Last of Gaelic monarchs of the Gael,
Slumbering by the young, eternal
River-voices of the western vale.

T. W. Rolleston

Abbey Asaroe

Gray, gray is Abbey Asaroe, by Belashanny town,
It has neither door nor window, the walls are
    broken down;
The carven-stones lie scattered in briar and
    nettle-bed;
The only feet are those that come at burial of the
    dead.
A little rocky rivulet runs murmuring to the tide,
Singing a song of ancient days, in sorrow, not in
    pride;
The boortree and the lightsome ash across the
    portal grow,
And heaven itself is now the roof of Abbey Asaroe.

It looks beyond the harbour-stream to Gulban
    mountain blue;
It hears the voice of Erna's fall,—Atlantic breakers
    too;
High ships go sailing past it; the sturdy clank of oars
Brings in the salmon-boat to haul a net upon the
    shores;
And this way to his home-creek, when the summer
    day is done,

Slow sculls the weary fisherman across the setting
    sun;
While green with corn is Sheegus Hill, his cottage
    white below;
But gray at every season is Abbey Asaroe.

There stood one day a poor old man above its
    broken bridge;
He heard no running rivulet, he saw no
    mountain-ridge;
He turned his back on Sheegus Hill and viewed
    with misty sight
The Abbey walls, the burial-ground with crosses
    ghostly white;
Under a weary weight of years he bowed upon his
    staff,
Perusing in the present time the former's epitaph;
For, gray and wasted like the walls, a figure full of
    woe,
This man was of the blood of them who founded
    Asaroe.

From Derry to Bundrowas Tower, Tirconnell
    broad was theirs;
Spearmen and plunder, bards and wine, and holy
    abbot's prayers;

With chanting always in the house which they had
    builded high
To God and to Saint Bernard,—where at last they
    came to die.
At worst, no workhouse grave for him! the ruins of
    his race
Shall rest among the ruin'd stones of this their
    saintly place.
The fond old man was weeping; and tremulous
    and slow
Along the rough and crooked lane he crept from
    Asaroe.

William Allingham

XIII
The Celts

Long, long ago, beyond the misty space
    Of twice a thousand years,
In Erin old there dwelt a mighty race,
    Taller than Roman spears;
Like oaks and towers they had a giant grace,
    Were fleet as deers,
With wind and waves they made their 'biding place,
    These western shepherd seers.

Their Ocean-God was Manannan, MacLir,
    Whose angry lips,
In their white foam, full often would inter
    Whole fleets of ships;
Cromah their Day-God, and their Thunderer
    Made morning and eclipse;
Bride was their Queen of Song, and unto her
    They prayed with fire-touched lips.

Great were their deeds, their passions and their
      sports;
    With clay and stone
They piled on strath and shore those mystic forts,
    Not yet o'erthrown;
On cairn-crowned hills they held their
      council-courts;
    While youths alone,
With giant dogs, explored the elk resorts,
    And brought them down.

Of these was Fin, the father of the Bard
    Whose ancient song
Over the clamour of all change is heard,
    Sweet-voiced and strong.
Fin once o'ertook Grania, the golden-haired,
    The fleet and young;

From her the lovely, and from him the feared,
    The primal poet sprung.

Ossian! two thousand years of mist and change
    Surround thy name—
Thy Finian heroes now no longer range
    The hills of fame.
The very names of Fin and Gaul sound strange—
    Yet thine the same—
By miscalled lake and desecrated grange—
    Remains, and shall remain!

The Druid's altar and the Druid's creed
    We scarce can trace,
There is not left an undisputed deed
    Of all your race,
Save your majestic song, which hath their speed,
    And strength and grace;
In that sole song, they live and love, and bleed—
    It bears them on through space.

O, inspired giant! shall we e'er behold,
    In our own time,
One fit to speak your spirit on the wold,
    Or seize your rhyme?
One pupil of the past, as mighty-souled
    As in the prime,

Were the fond, fair, and beautiful, and bold—
　　They, of your song sublime!

Thomas D'Arcy McGee

XIV
Ode

We are the music-makers,
　　And we are the dreamers of dreams,
Wandering by lone sea-breakers,
　　And sitting by desolate streams;—
World-losers and world-forsakers,
　　On whom the pale moon gleams:
Yet we are the movers and shakers
　　Of the world for ever, it seems.

With wonderful deathless ditties
We build up the world's great cities,
　　And out of a fabulous story
　　We fashion an empire's glory:
One man with a dream, at pleasure,
　　Shall go forth and conquer a crown;
And three with a new song's measure
　　Can trample a kingdom down.

We, in the ages lying
  In the buried past of the earth,
Built Nineveh with our sighing,
  And Babel itself in our mirth;
And o'erthrew them with prophesying
  To the old of the new world's worth;
For each age is a dream that is dying,
  Or one that is coming to birth.

Arthur O'Shaughnessy

XV

Strings in the Earth and Air

Strings in the earth and air
  Make music sweet;
Strings by the river where
  The willows meet.

There's music along the river
  For Love wanders there,
Pale flowers on his mantle,
  Dark leaves on his hair.

All softly playing,
    With head to the music bent,
And fingers straying
    Upon an instrument.

James Joyce

XVI

Over My Head the Forest Wall

Over my head the forest wall
Rises; the ousel sings to me;
Above my booklet lined for words
The woodland birds shake out their glee.
There's the blithe cuckoo chanting clear
In mantle grey from bough to bough;
God keep me still! For here I write
His gospel bright in great woods now.

Robin Flower
(From the Irish)

The Making of Birds

God made Him birds in a pleasant humour;
　　Tired of planets and suns was He.
He said: "I will add a glory to summer,
　　Gifts for my creatures banished from Me!"

He had a thought and it set Him smiling
　　Of the shape of a bird and its glancing head,
Its dainty air and its grace beguiling:
　　"I will make feathers," the Lord God said.

He made the robin; He made the swallow;
　　His deft hands moulding the shape to His mood,
The thrush and the lark and the finch to follow,
　　And laughed to see that His work was good.

He Who has given men gift of laughter,
　　Made in His image; He fashioned fit
The blink of the owl and the stork thereafter,
　　The little wren and the long-tailed tit.

He spent in the making His wit and fancies;
　　The wing-feathers He fashioned them strong;
Deft and dear as daisies and pansies,
　　He crowned His work with the gift of song.

"Dearlings," He said, "make songs for My praises!"
  He tossed them loose to the sun and wind,
Airily sweet as pansies and daisies;
  He taught them to build a nest to their mind.

The dear Lord God of His glories weary—
  Christ our Lord had the heart of a boy—
Made Him birds in a moment merry,
  Bade them soar and sing for His joy.

Katharine Tynan

XVIII

My Hope, My Love

My hope, my love, we will go
Into the woods, scattering the dews,
Where we will behold the salmon, and the ousel in
    its nest,
The deer and the roe-buck calling,
The sweetest bird on the branches warbling,
The cuckoo on the summit of the green hill;
And death shall never approach us
In the bosom of the fragrant wood!

Edward Walsh
(From the Irish)

The Lover and Birds

Within a budding grove,
In April's ear sang every bird his best,
But not a song to pleasure my unrest,
Or touch the tears unwept of bitter love.
Some spake, methought, with pity, some as if in jest.
      To every word
      Of every bird
I listened, and replied as it behove.

Screamed Chaffinch, "Sweet, sweet, sweet!
Pretty lovey, come and meet me here!"
"Chaffinch," quoth I, "be dumb awhile, in fear
Thy darling prove no better than a cheat,
And never come, or fly when wintry days appear."
      Yet from a twig
      With voice so big,
The little fowl his utterance did repeat.

Then I, "The man forlorn
Hears Earth send up a foolish noise aloft."
"And what'll *he* do? what'll *he* do?" scoffed
The Blackbird, standing in an ancient thorn,

Then spread his sooty wings and flitted to the
croft
With cackling laugh:
Whom I, being half
Enraged, called after, giving back his scorn.
Worse mocked the Thrush, "Die! die!
Oh, could he do it? could he do it? Nay!
Be quick! be quick! Here, here, here!" (went
his lay)
"Take heed! take heed!" then, "Why? why?
why? why? why?
See-ee now! see-ee now!" (he drawled). "Back!
back! back! R-r-r-run away!"
O Thrush, be still!
Or, at thy will,
See some less sad interpreter than I.

"Air, air! blue air and white!
Whither I flee, whither, O whither, O whither
I flee!"
(Thus the Lark hurried, mounting from the
lea)
"Hills, countries, many waters glittering
bright,
Whither I see, whither I see! deeper, deeper,
deeper, whither I see, see, see!"

"Gay Lark," I said,
      "The song that's bred
In happy nest may well to heaven make
      flight."

"There's something, something sad,
   I half remember"—piped a broken strain.
Well sung, sweet Robin! Robin sung again,
   "Spring's opening cheerily, cheerily! be we
      glad!"
Which moved, I wist not why, me melancholy mad,
         Till now, grown meek,
         With wetted cheek,
Most comforting and gentle thoughts I had.

                                    William Allingham

                    XX

            Fly to the Desert

Fly to the desert, fly with me,
Our Arab tents are rude for thee;
But oh! the choice what heart can doubt,
Of tents with love, or thrones without?

                    27

Our rocks are rough, but smiling there
The acacia waves her yellow hair.
Lonely and sweet, nor loved the less
For flowering in a wilderness.

Our sands are bare, but down their slope
The silvery-footed antelope
As gracefully and gaily springs
As o'er the marble courts of kings.

Then come—thy Arab maid will be
The loved and lone acacia tree,
The antelope, whose feet shall bless
With their light sound thy loneliness.

Thomas Moore

XXI

A Twilight in Middle March

Within the oak a throb of pigeon wings
Fell silent, and grey twilight hushed the fold,
And spiders' hammocks swung on half-oped
   things
That shook like foreigners upon our cold.
A gipsy lit a fire and made a sound
Of moving tins, and from an oblong moon

The river seemed to gush across the ground
To the cracked metre of a marching tune.

And then three syllables of melody
Dropped from a blackbird's flute, and died apart
Far in the dewy dark. No more but three,
Yet sweeter music never touched a heart
'Neath the blue domes of London. Flute and reed
Suggested feelings of the solitude
When will was all the Delphi I would heed,
Lost like a wind within a summer wood
From little knowledge where great sorrows brood.

Francis Ledwidge

XXII

Flower-Quiet in the Rush-Strewn Sheiling

Flower-quiet in the rush-strewn sheiling
At the dawntime Grainne lay,
While beneath the birch-toppled roof the sunlight
Groped upon its way
And stooped over her sleeping white body
With a wasp-yellow ray.

The hot breath of the day awoke her,
And wearied of its heat

She wandered out by noisy elms
On the cool mossy peat,
Where the shadowed leaves like pecking linnets
Nodded around her feet.

She leaned and saw in pale grey waters,
By twisted hazel boughs,
Her lips like heavy drooping poppies
In a rich redness drowse,
Then swallow-lightly touched the ripples
Until her wet lips were
Burning as ripened rowan berries
Through the white winter air.

Lazily she lingered
Gazing so,
As the slender osiers
Where the waters flow,
As green twigs of sally
Swaying to and fro.
Sleepy moths fluttered
In her dark eyes,
And her lips grew quieter
Than lullabies.
Swaying with the reedgrass
Over the stream

Lazily she lingered
Cradling a dream.

A brown bird rises
Out of the marshes,
By sallow pools flying
On winds from the sea,
By pebbly rivers,
Tired of the salt gusts
Sweetly 'twill whistle
On a mountainy tree.
So, gladdened, impulsive,
Grainne arising
Sped through the bluebells
Under the branches,
White by the alders
Glimmering she
Stole in the shadows,
Flashing through sunshine,
Her feet like the raindrops
On withered leaves falling
Lightful and free.

She stood beyond the reddening hawthorns
Out in the wild air
And gathering back with white-lit fingers

Her wind-loosened hair,
She scanned the dark bog-waters
Sleeping beneath the bare
Turf banks and the wide brown marshes,
But she could only find
The froth-pale blossom of the boglands
As it fluttered on the waves of the wandering wind
So she came, a little saddened,
Bending with the slim breeze
Through the elm-misted sunshine
And flowers like pools of blue seas.
Quiet as her breath she glided
In the grass-green shade of trees.

A bird sang like a rainy well.
Then on a fallen bough
A hurrying footstep spoke, and Diarmuid
Stood before her now,
Sunburnt, pine-straight, the hilly breezes
Upon his lips and brow.

Austin Clarke

Paean of Dawn in May

In the darkness before dawn
When dews make grey the field
And the world is trance-withdrawn
And trees but half revealed,
O then, high up, above the topmost lawn,
What fountains are unsealed!

Scarce can the eye see light
When the ear becomes aware
That instruments exquisite
Are raining from the air,
While sun and pale moon mingle their delight,
Adorations everywhere!

Who are these solemnising
In song-mists crystalline
Between the sun's uprising
And the sheenèd moon's decline
Glories so far above our poor devising
Unseen before the shrine?

Whose are these rainbow-hued
Symphonies high and higher
Wafted in multitude

Of choir outclimbing choir,
As though the heavens were some deep-tangled
    wood
And each leaf voice and fire?

Eddy of golden dust
Halo of rays
Thrilling up, up, as they must
Die of the life they praise.
The larks! the larks! that to the earth entrust
Only their sleeping-place.

Hark! it grows less and less,
That rapture nothing mars;
They rise beyond our guess
Beyond our senses' bars,
They drink the virgin Light, the measureless,
And in it fade like stars.

Earth sends them up from hills—
Her wingèd wishes, they!
Wild hopes, that nothing kills,
To outsoar the young Day,
To shake off all that chains the soul and chills
In one immortal ray!

They ascend ere the first beam
On dark heaven waxes strong
To dwell in that blue stream
Of Dawn, and float along—
The zenith and the future all their dream—
And the world's roofed with song!

Herbert Trench

XXIV
Anacreontic

When spring came on with fresh delight,
To cheer the soul and charm the sight,
While easy breezes, softer rain,
And warmer suns, salute the plain,
'Twas then in yonder piny grove,
That Nature went to meet with Love.

   Green was her robe, and green her wreath,
Where'er she trod 'twas green beneath;
Where'er she turn'd the pulses beat
With new recruits of genial heat;
And in her train the birds appear,
To match for all the coming year.

   Rais'd on a bank, where daisies grew,

And vi'lets intermixed a blue,
She finds the boy she went to find;
A thousand Pleasures wait behind;
Aside a thousand arrows lie,
But all unfeather'd wait to fly.

   When they met, the dame and boy,
Dancing Graces, idle Joy,
Wanton Smiles, and airy Play,
Conspir'd to make the scene be gay;
Love pair'd the birds through all the grove,
And Nature bid them sing to Love;
Sitting, hopping, flutt'ring, sing,
And pay their tribute from the wing.
To fledge the shafts that idly lie,
And yet unfeather'd wait to fly.

   'Tis thus, when spring renews the blood,
They meet in ev'ry trembling wood,
And thrice they make the plumes agree,
And ev'ry dart they mount with three,
And ev'ry dart can boast a kind,
Which suits each proper turn of mind.

   From the tow'ring eagle's plume
The gen'rous hearts accept their doom;
Shot by the peacock's painted eye,
The vain and airy lovers die:

For careful dames and frugal men
The shafts are speckled by the hen.
The pyes and parrots deck the darts,
When prattling wins the panting hearts;
When from the voice the passions spring,
The warbling finch affords a wing:
Together by the sparrow stung,
Down fall the wanton and the young;
And fledg'd by geese the weapons fly,
When others love they know not why.

    All this (as late I chanced to rove)
I learned in yonder waving grove.
"And see," says Love (who call'd me near)
"How much I deal with Nature here,
How both support a proper part,
She gives the feather, I the dart:
Then cease for souls averse to sigh,
If Nature cross ye, so do I;
My weapon there unfeather'd flies,
And shakes and shuffles through the skies:
But if the mutual charms I find
By which she links you mind to mind,
They wing my shafts, I poize the darts,
And strike from both through both your hearts."

Thomas Parnell

In the Cathedral Close

In the Dean's porch a nest of clay
  With five small tenants may be seen,
Five solemn faces, each as wise
  As though its owner were a Dean;

Five downy fledglings in a row,
  Packed close, as in the antique pew
The schoolgirls are whose foreheads clear
  At the *Venite* shine on you.

Day after day the swallows sit
  With scarce a stir, with scarce a sound,
But dreaming and digesting much
  They grow thus wise and soft and round.

They watch the Canons come to dine,
  And hear, the mullion-bars across,
Over the fragrant fruit and wine
  Deep talk of rood-screen and reredos.

Her hands with field-flowers drenched, a child
  Leaps past in wind-blown dress and hair,
The swallows turn their heads askew—
  Five judges deem that she is fair.

Prelusive touches sound within,
  Straightway they recognise the sign,
And, blandly nodding, they approve
  The minuet of Rubinstein.

They mark the cousins' schoolboy talk,
  (Male birds flown wide from minster bell)
And blink at each broad term of art,
  Binomial or bicycle.

Ah! downy young ones, soft and warm,
  Doth such a stillness mask from sight
Such swiftness? can such peace conceal
  Passion and ecstasy of flight?

Yet somewhere 'mid your Eastern suns,
  Under a white Greek architrave
At morn, or when the shaft of fire
  Lies large upon the Indian wave,

A sense of something dear gone-by
  Will stir, strange longings thrill the heart
For a small world embowered and close,
  Of which ye some time were a part.

The dew-drench'd flowers, the child's glad eyes,
  Your joy unhuman shall control,

And in your wings a light and wind
  Shall move from the Maestro's soul.

Edward Dowden

XXVI

Golden Stockings

Golden stockings you had on
In the meadow where you ran;
And your little knees together
Bobbed like pippins in the weather
When the breezes rush and fight
For those dimples of delight;
And they dance from the pursuit,
And the leaf looks like the fruit.

I have many a sight in mind
That would last if I were blind;
Many verses I could write
That would bring me many a sight.
Now I only see but one,
See you running in the sun;
And the gold-dust coming up
From the trampled butter-cup.

Oliver Gogarty

Child's Song

I have a garden of my own,
  Shining with flowers of every hue;
I loved it dearly while alone,
  But I shall love it more with you:
And there the golden bees shall come,
  In summer time at break of morn,
And wake us with their busy hum
  Around the Siha's fragrant thorn.

I have a fawn from Aden's land,
  On leafy buds and berries nurst;
And you shall feed him from your hand,
  Though he may start with fear at first.
And I will lead you where he lies
  For shelter from the noon-tide heat;
And you may touch his sleeping eyes,
  And feel his little silv'ry feet.

                              Thomas Moore

XXVIII

The County Mayo

Now with the coming in of the spring the days
    will stretch a bit,
And after the Feast of Brigid I shall hoist my flag
    and go,
For since the thought got into my head I can
    neither stand nor sit
Until I find myself in the middle of the County of
    Mayo.

In Claremorris I would stop a night and sleep
    with decent men,
And then go on to Balla just beyond and drink
    galore,
And next to Kiltimagh for a visit of about a
    month, and then
I would only be a couple of miles away from
    Ballymore.

I say and swear my heart lifts up like the lifting of
    a tide,
Rising up like the rising wind till fog or mist
    must go,
When I remember Carra and Gallen close beside,

And the Gap of the Two Bushes, and the wide
    plains of Mayo.

To Killaden then, to the place where everything
    grows that is best,
There are raspberries there and strawberries there
    and all that is good for men;
And if I were only there in the middle of my folk
    my heart could rest,
For age itself would leave me there and I'd be
    young again.

                 James Stephens
            (From the Irish of Raftery)

XXIX
Larks

All day in exquisite air
The song clomb an invisible stair,
Flight on flight, story on story,
Into the dazzling glory.

There was no bird, only a singing,
Up in the glory, climbing and ringing,
Like a small golden cloud at even,
Trembling 'twixt earth and heaven.

I saw no staircase winding, winding,
Up in the dazzle, sapphire and blinding,
Yet round by round, in exquisite air,
The song went up the stair.

Katharine Tynan

The Beggar's Child

Mavourneen, we'll go far away
From the net of the crooked town,
Where they grudge us the light of the day.

Around my neck you will lay
Two tight little arms of brown.
  Mavourneen, we'll go far away
  From the net of the crooked town.

And what will we hear on the way?
The stir of wings up and down, says she,
In nests where the little birds stay!
  Mavourneen, we'll go far away
  From the net of the crooked town,
  Where they grudge us the light of the day.

Padraic Colum

Epitaph

Where she fell swearing, hand to side,
   The old tramp woman lies.
For every bitter year of her life
   A raven flies,
And the black ungainly procession
   Flaps over the skies.

L. A. G. Strong

Solstice

The day is tired with idlenesse and awe.
The fishing-boats stand fixed along the sea.
Upon the heather hangs the drowsy bee
O'ercome with sweetness. Even within the claw
Of yonder bird the tettix fills his maw,
And burns with gold and crimson. Silently
A reaper passes dreamlike. Creatures free
Within the prisoning heat and this one law—
         The day is tired.

The sun stands still upon the livid sky;
And the great mountains go up to it there,
Fable on wondrous fable; and the air
Pulses with flame and darkness everywhere
—Or only in my brain, upon mine eye,
And still about my forehead and my hair.
                    The day is tired.

Charles Weekes

XXXIII

The Fountain

The fountain falls from laughing mouth of stone
In crescent laughter thro' the scented gloom
And from the corner of the curved lip
The drops like petals gather, fall, and slip
From carven leaf to leaf. I am alone
By the slim, white, unwitherable plume
The water flaunts against a deathless sky.
And I, who found in mutability
A little music and a little laughter,
See there before me Beauty's strange hereafter,
The immortal ghost, too gay, too sad, to die.

H. Stuart

"In the Midst of Life . . ."

All the long day the robin on the spray
    Piped his sweet song
To her who on her hidden nest
Oft turned beneath her patient breast
Her pretty eggs in tender quest
    All the long day.

All the long day the blossoms on the spray
    Shook 'neath his song.
Kissed by the sun each petal curled
To perfect flower, its bloom unfurled
To fling fine incense to the world
    All the day long.

All the long day there passed me on their way
    A busy throng—
The laden bee to her abode,
The toiling ant who drew her load
Across the danger of the road
    All the day long.

All the long day I heard from far away
    A slow ding-dong;
Within the vale the village lies

All still beneath the smiling skies,
Save this sad bell that swings and cries
All the day long.

Dora Sigerson Shorter

XXXV

The Stolen Child

Where dips the rocky highland
Of Sleuth Wood in the lake,
There lies a leafy island
Where flapping herons wake
The drowsy water rats;
There we've hid our faery vats,
Full of berries,
And of reddest stolen cherries.
Come away, O human child!
To the waters and the wild
With a faery, hand in hand,
For the world's more full of weeping than you can
understand.

Where the wave of moonlight glosses
The dim gray sands with light,
Far off by farthest Rosses

We foot it all the night,
Weaving olden dances,
Mingling hands and mingling glances
Till the moon has taken flight;
To and fro we leap
And chase the frothy bubbles,
While the world is full of troubles
And is anxious in its sleep.
Come away, O human child!
To the waters and the wild
With a faery, hand in hand,
For the world's more full of weeping than you can
    understand.

Where the wandering water gushes
From the hills above Glen-Car,
In pools among the rushes
That scarce could bathe a star,
We seek for slumbering trout
And whispering in their ears
Give them unquiet dreams;
Leaning softly out
From ferns that drop their tears
Over the young streams,
Come away, O human child!
To the waters and the wild

With a faery, hand in hand,
For the world's more full of weeping than you can
    understand.

Away with us he's going,
The solemn-eyed:
He'll hear no more the lowing
Of the calves on the warm hillside
Or the kettle on the hob
Sing peace into his breast,
Or see the brown mice bob
Round and round the oatmeal-chest.
For he comes, the human child,
To the waters and the wild
With a faery, hand in hand,
From a world more full of weeping than he can
    understand.

W. B. Yeats

XXXVI

The Goat Paths

The crooked paths go every way
    Upon the hill—they wind about
    Through the heather in and out

Of the quiet sunniness.
And there the goats, day after day,
    Stray in sunny quietness,
Cropping here and cropping there,
    As they pause and turn and pass,
Now a bit of heather spray,
    Now a mouthful of the grass.

In the deeper sunniness,
    In the place where nothing stirs,
Quietly in quietness,
    In the quiet of the furze,
For a time they come and lie
Staring on the roving sky.
If you approach they run away,
    They leap and stare, away they bound,
    With a sudden angry sound,
To the sunny quietude;
    Crouching down where nothing stirs
    In the silence of the furze,
Crouching down again to brood
In the sunny solitude.

If I were as wise as they
    I would stray apart and brood,
I would beat a hidden way

Through the quiet heather spray
  To a sunny solitude;
And should you come I'd run away,
  I would make an angry sound,
  I would stare and turn and bound
To the deeper quietude,
  To the place where nothing stirs
  In the silence of the furze.
In that airy quietness
  I would think as long as they;
Through the quiet sunniness
  I would stray away to brood
By a hidden beaten way
  In a sunny solitude.

I would think until I found
  Something I can never find,
Something lying on the ground,
  In the bottom of my mind.

James Stephens

XXXVII

The Wedding of the Clans

A Girl's Babble

I go to knit two clans together;
  Our clan and this clan unseen of yore:—
Our clan fears nought! but I go, O whither?
  This day I go from my mother's door.

Thou, red-breast, singest the old song over,
  Though many a time thou hast sung it before;
They never sent thee to some strange lover:—
  I sing a new song by my mother's door.

I stepped from my little room down by the ladder,
  The ladder that never so shook before;
I was sad last night; to-day I am sadder,
  Because I go from my mother's door.

The last snow melts upon bush and bramble;
  The gold bars shine on the forest's floor;
Shake not, thou leaf! it is I must tremble
  Because I go from my mother's door.

From a Spanish sailor a dagger I bought me;
    I trailed a rose-tree our grey bawn o'er;
The creed and my letters our old bard taught me;
    My days were sweet by my mother's door.

My little white goat that with raised feet huggest
    The oak stock, thy horns in the ivies frore,
Could I wrestle like thee—how the wreaths thou
      tuggest!—
    I never would move from my mother's door.

O weep no longer, my nurse and mother!
    My foster sister, weep not so sore!
You cannot come with me, Ir, my brother—
    Alone I go from my mother's door.

Farewell, my wolf-hound that slew MacOwing
    As he caught me and far through the thickets
      bore:
My heifer, Alb, in the green vale lowing,
    My cygnet's nest upon Lorna's shore!

He has killed ten chiefs, this chief that plights me,
    His hand is like that of the giant Balor;
But I fear his kiss, and his beard affrights me,
    And the great stone dragon above his door.

Had I daughters nine, with me they should tarry;
　　They should sing old songs; they should dance
　　　　at my door;
They should grind at the quern;—no need to
　　　　marry;
　　O when will this marriage day be o'er?

Had I buried, like Moirín, three mates already,
　　I might say: "Three husbands! then why not
　　　　four?"
But my hand is cold and my foot unsteady,
　　Because I never was married before!

Aubrey de Vere

XXXVIII

The County of Mayo

On the deck of Patrick Lynch's boat I sat in
　　woeful plight,
Through my singing all the weary day, and
　　weeping all the night.
Were it not that full of sorrow from my people
　　forth I go,
By the blessed sun! 'tis royally I'd sing thy praise,
　　Mayo!

When I dwelt at home in plenty, and my gold did
      much abound,
In the company of fair young maids the Spanish
      ale went round—
'Tis a bitter change from those gay days that now
      I'm forced to go,
And must leave my bones in Santa Cruz, far from
      my own Mayo.

They are altered girls in Irrul now; 'tis proud
      they're grown and high,
With their hair-bags and their top-knots—for I
      pass their buckles by;
But it's little now I heed their airs, for God will
      have it so,
That I must depart for foreign lands, and leave
      my sweet Mayo.

'Tis my grief that Patrick Loughlin is not Earl of
      Irrul still,
And that Brian Duff no longer rules as Lord upon
      the hill,
And that Colonel Hugh MacGrady should be
      lying dead and low,

And I sailing, sailing swiftly from the county of
Mayo.

George Fox
(From the Irish)

XXXIX

Adieu to Belashanny

Adieu to Belashanny! where I was bred and born;
Go where I may, I'll think of you, as sure as night
and morn.
The kindly spot, the friendly town, where every
one is known,
And not a face in all the place but partly seems
my own;
There's not a house or window, there's not a field
or hill,
But, east or west, in foreign lands, I'll recollect
them still.
I leave my warm heart with you, tho' my back I'm
forced to turn—
Adieu to Belashanny, and the winding banks of
Erne!

No more on pleasant evenings we'll saunter down
the Mall,
When the trout is rising to the fly, the salmon to
the fall.
The boat comes straining on her net, and heavily
she creeps,
Cast off, cast off—she feels the oars, and to her
berth she sweeps;
Now fore and aft keep hauling, and gathering up
the clew,
Till a silver wave of salmon rolls in among the
crew.
Then they may sit, with pipes a-lit, and many a
joke and "yarn";—
Adieu to Belashanny, and the winding banks of
Erne!

The music of the waterfall, the mirror of the tide,
When all the green-hill'd harbour is full from side
to side,
From Portnasun to Bulliebawns, and round the
Abbey Bay,
From rocky Inis Saimer to Coolnargit sand-hills
grey;
While far upon the southern line, to guard it like a
wall,

The Leitrim mountains clothed in blue gaze
    calmly over all,
And watch the ship sail up or down, the red flag
    at her stern;—
Adieu to these, adieu to all the winding banks of
    Erne!

Farewell to you, Kildoney lads, and them that pull
    an oar,
A lug-sail set, or haul a net, from the Point to
    Mullaghmore;
From Killybegs to bold Slieve-League, that
    ocean-mountain steep,
Six hundred yards in air aloft, six hundred in the
    deep;
From Dooran to the Fairy Bridge, and round by
    Tullen strand,
Level and long, and white with waves, where gull
    and curlew stand;
Head out to sea when on your lee the breakers
    you discern!—
Adieu to all the billowy coast, and winding banks
    of Erne!

Farewell, Coolmore,—Bundoran! and your
    summer crowds that run

From inland homes to see with joy th' Atlantic-
    setting sun;

To breathe the buoyant salted air, and sport
    among the waves;

To gather shells on sandy beach, and tempt the
    gloomy caves;

To watch the flowing, ebbing tide, the boats, the
    crabs, the fish;

Young men and maids to meet and smile, and
    form a tender wish;

The sick and old in search of health, for all things
    have their turn—

And I must quit my native shore, and the winding
    banks of Erne!

Farewell to every white cascade from the Harbour
    to Belleek,

And every pool where fins may rest, and ivy-
    shaded creek;

The sloping fields, the lofty rocks, where ash and
    holly grow,

The one split yew-tree gazing on the curving flood
    below;

The Lough, that winds through islands under
   Turaw mountain green;
And Castle Caldwell's stretching woods, with
   tranquil bays between;
And Breesie Hill, and many a pond among the
   heath and fern,—
For I must say adieu—adieu to the winding banks
   of Erne!

The thrush will call through Camlin groves the
   live-long summer day;
The waters run by mossy cliff, and banks with
   wild flowers gay;
The girls will bring their work and sing beneath a
   twisted thorn,
Or stray with sweethearts down the path among
   the growing corn;
Along the river-side they go, where I have often
   been,
O, never shall I see again the days that I have
   seen!
A thousand chances are to one I never may return,—
Adieu to Belashanny, and the winding banks of
   Erne!

Adieu to evening dances, when merry neighbours
    meet,
And the fiddle says to boys and girls, "Get up and
    shake your feet!"
To "shanachus" and wise old talk of Erin's days
    gone by—
Who trench'd the rath on such a hill, and where
    the bones may lie
Of saint, or king, or warrior chief; with tales of
    fairy power,
And tender ditties sweetly sung to pass the
    twilight hour.
The mournful song of exile is now for me to learn—
Adieu, my dear companions on the winding banks
    of Erne!

Now measure from the Commons down to each
    end of the Purt,
Round the Abbey, Moy, and Knather,—I wish no
    one any hurt;
The Main Street, Back Street, College Lane, the
    Mall, and Portnasun,
If any foes of mine are there, I pardon every one.
I hope that man and womankind will do the same
    by me;

For my heart is sore and heavy at voyaging the
    sea.
My loving friends I'll bear in mind, and often
    fondly turn
To think of Belashanny and the winding banks of
    Erne.

If ever I'm a money'd man, I mean, please God,
    to cast
My golden anchor in the place where youthful
    years were pass'd;
Though heads that now are black and brown must
    meanwhile gather gray,
New faces rise by every hearth, and old ones
    drop away—
Yet dearer still that Irish hill than all the world
    beside;
It's home, sweet home, where'er I roam, through
    lands and waters wide.
And if the Lord allows me, I surely will return
To my native Belashanny, and the winding banks
    of Erne.

William Allingham

The Village

Sweet was the sound, when oft at evening's close
Up yonder hill the village murmur rose;
There, as I passed with careless steps and slow,
The mingling notes came soften'd from below:
The swain responsive as the milkmaid sung,
The sober herd that low'd to meet their young;
The noisy geese that gabbled o'er the pool,
The playful children just let loose from school;
The watchdog's voice that bay'd the whisp'ring
    wind,
And the loud laugh that spoke the vacant mind;
These all in sweet confusion sought the shade,
And fill'd each pause the nightingale had made.
But now the sounds of population fail,
No cheerful murmurs fluctuate in the gale,
No busy steps the grass-grown footway tread,
For all the bloomy flush of life is fled.
All but yon widow'd, solitary thing,
That feebly bends beside the plashy spring:
She, wretched matron, forc'd in age, for bread,
To strip the brook with mantling cresses spread,
To strip her wintry faggot from the thorn,

To seek her nightly shed, and weep till morn;
She only left of all the harmless train,
The sad historian of the pensive plain.

Oliver Goldsmith

Lament of the Irish Emigrant

I'm sitting on the stile, Mary,
  Where we sat side by side
On a bright May morning, long ago,
  When first you were my bride;
The corn was springing fresh and green,
  And the lark sang loud and high—
And the red was on your lip, Mary,
  And the love-light in your eye.

The place is little changed, Mary,
  The day is bright as then,
The lark's loud song is in my ear,
  And the corn is green again;
But I miss the soft clasp of your hand,
  And your breath, warm on my cheek,
And I still keep listening for the words
  You never more will speak.

'Tis but a step down yonder lane,
   And the little church stands near—
The church where we were wed, Mary,
   I see the spire from here.
But the grave-yard lies between, Mary,
   And my step might break your rest—
For I've laid you, darling! down to sleep,
   With your baby on your breast.

I'm very lonely now, Mary,
   For the poor make no new friends,
But, oh! they love the better still,
   The few our Father sends!
And you were all I had, Mary,
   My blessing and my pride!
There's nothing left to care for now,
   Since my poor Mary died.

I'm bidding you a long farewell,
   My Mary—kind and true!
But I'll not forget you, darling,
   In the land I'm going to:
They say there's bread and work for all,
   And the sun shines always there—
But I'll not forget old Ireland,
   Were it fifty times as fair!

And often in those grand old woods
   I'll sit and shut my eyes,
And my heart will travel back again
   To the place where Mary lies;
And I'll think I see the little stile
   Where we sat side by side,
And the springing corn and the bright May morn
   When first you were my bride.

Lady Dufferin

XLII

A Peasant Woman's Song
1864

I'm very happy where I am,
   Far across the say,
I'm very happy far from home,
   In North Amerikay.

It's lonely in the night when Pat
   Is sleeping by my side,
I lie awake, and no one knows
   The big tears that I've cried;

For a little voice still calls me back
   To my far, far countrie,
And nobody can hear it spake.
   Oh! nobody but me.

There is a little spot of ground
   Behind the chapel wall,
It's nothing but a tiny mound,
   Without a stone at all;

It rises in my heart just now,
   It makes a dawny hill;
It's from below the voice comes out,
   I cannot keep it still.

Oh! little Voice; ye call me back
   To my far, far countrie,
And nobody can hear ye spake,
   Oh! nobody but me.

Dion Boucicault

My Grief on the Sea

My grief on the sea,
  How the waves of it roll!
For they heave between me
  And the love of my soul!

Abandoned, forsaken,
  To grief and to care,
Will the sea ever waken
  Relief from despair?

My grief, and my trouble!
  Would he and I were
In the province of Leinster
  Or County of Clare.

Were I and my darling—
  Oh, heart-bitter wound!—
On board of the ship
  For America bound.

On a green bed of rushes
  All last night I lay,
And I flung it abroad
  With the heat of the day.

And my love came behind me—
    He came from the South;
His breast to my bosom,
    His mouth to my mouth.

Douglas Hyde
(From the Irish)

XLIV

Johnny's the Lad I Love

As I roved out on a May morning,
Being in the youthful spring,
I leaned my back close to the garden wall
To hear the small birds sing;

And to hear two lovers talk, my dear,
To know what they would say,
That I might know a little of her mind
Before I would go away.

"Come sit you down, my heart," he says,
"All on this pleasant green,
It's full three-quarters of a year and more
Since together you and I have been."

"I will not sit on the grass," she said,
"Now nor any other time,
For I hear you're engaged with another maid,
And your heart is no more of mine.

"Oh, I'll not believe what an old man says,
For his days are well nigh done.
Nor will I believe what a young man says,
For he's fair to many a one.

"But I will climb a high, high tree,
And rob a wild bird's nest,
And I'll bring back whatever I do find
To the arms I love the best," she said,
"To the arms I love the best."

Anonymous

XLV

O Youth of the Bound Black Hair

O Youth of the bound black hair,
With whom I was once together.
You went by this way last night,
And you did not come to see me.
I thought no harm would be done you
If you were to come and to ask for me,

71

And sure it is your little kiss would give comfort
If I were in the midst of a fever.

And I thought, my storeen,
That you were the sun and moon,
And I thought after that
That you were snow on the mountain,
And I thought after that
That you were a lamp from God,
Or that you were the star of knowledge
Going before me and after me.

Douglas Hyde
(From the Irish)

Mary Hynes

There is a sweet air on the side of the hill
When you are looking down upon Baile-laoi;
When you are walking in the valley picking nuts
      and blackberries
There is music of the birds in it and music of the
      sidhe.
What is the worth of greatness till you have the
      light

Of the flower of the branch that is by your side?
There is no good to deny it or to try to hide it,
She is the sun in the heavens who wounded my
  heart.

There is no part of Ireland I did not travel
From the rivers to the tops of the mountains,
To the edge of Loch Greine whose mouth is
  hidden,
And I saw no beauty but was behind hers.

Her hair was shining and her brows were shining
  too;
Her face was like herself, her mouth pleasant and
  sweet.
She is my pride, and I give her the branch,
She is the shining flower of Baile-laoi.

Lady Gregory
(From the Irish of Raftery)

Peggy Mitchell

As lily grows up easily,
In modest, gentle dignity
To sweet perfection,
So grew she,
As easily.

Or as the rose that takes no care
Will open out on sunny air
Bloom after bloom, fair after fair,
Sweet after sweet;
Just so did she,
As carelessly.

She is our torment without end,
She is our enemy and friend,
Our joy, our woe;
And she will send
Madness or glee
To you and me,
And endlessly.

James Stephens
(From the Irish of Raftery)

The Stars Stand up in the Air

The stars stand up in the air,
The sun and the moon are gone,
The strand of its waters is bare,
And her sway is swept from the swan.

The cuckoo was calling all day,
Hid in the branches above,
How my stórín is fled away,
'Tis my grief that I gave her my love.

Three things through love I see—
Sorrow and sin and death—
And my mind reminding me
That this doom I breathe with my breath.

But sweeter than violin or lute
Is my love—and she left me behind.
I wish that all music were mute,
And I to all beauty were blind.

She's more shapely than swan by the strand,
She's more radiant than grass after dew,
She's more fair than the stars where they stand—
'Tis my grief that her ever I knew!

Thomas MacDonagh
(From the Irish)

XLIX
Down by the Salley Gardens

Down by the salley gardens my love and I did
    meet;
She passed the salley gardens with little snow-
    white feet.
She bid me take love easy, as the leaves grow on
    the tree;
But I, being young and foolish, with her would
    not agree.

In a field by the river my love and I did stand,
And on my leaning shoulder she laid her
    snow-white hand.
She bid me take life easy, as the grass grows on
    the weirs;

But I was young and foolish, and now am full of
   tears.

W. B. Yeats

L

Love on the Mountain

My love comes down from the mountain
   Through the mists of dawn;
I look, and the star of the morning
   From the sky is gone.

My love comes down from the mountain,
   At dawn, dewy-sweet;
Did you step from the star to the mountain,
   O little white feet?

O whence came your twining tresses
   And your shining eyes,
But out of the gold of the morning
   And the blue of the skies?

The misty mountain is burning
   In the sun's red fire,
And the heart in my breast is burning
   And lost in desire.

I follow you into the valley
    But no word can I say;
To the East or the West I will follow
    Till the dusk of my day.

Thomas Boyd

LI

We will not Die, These Lovers Say

We will not die, these lovers say,
For any eyes but eyes of blue;
No hair shall win our hearts away
But hair of golden hue.

It is not with me as with those,
And yet a wiser song I sing,
Whom a love-lighted eye can please
Black as the raven's wing.

I ask no roses in her face,
No golden shimmer in her hair;
A pallid cheek for me has grace
And jet-black locks are fair.

Dark was the mother of that maid
Who brought proud Ilion to its fall;

Yet shining locks of golden braid
Had Helen fair and tall.

Which was the lovelier of the two
—Red-lipped, sweet-voiced that winsome pair—
There was no man on earth that knew,
The dark one or the fair.

Robin Flower
(From the Irish of Richard Burke)

LII

Two Generations

I turned and gave my strength to woman
Instead of to the unwilling field.
Sinew and soul are gone to win her,
Slow, and most perilous, her yield.

The son I got stood up beside me,
With fire and quiet beauty filled:
He looked on me, and then he looked
Upon the field I had not tilled.

He kissed me, and went forth to labour
Where lonely tilth and moorland meet,

A gull above the ploughshare hears
The ironic song of our defeat.

L. A. G. Strong

Will You Be as Hard?

Will you be as hard,
    Colleen, as you are quiet?
Will you be without pity
    On me for ever?

Listen to me, Noireen,
    Listen, aroon;
Put healing on me
    From your quiet mouth.

I am in the little road
    That is dark and narrow,
The little road that has led
    Thousands to sleep.

Lady Gregory
(From the Irish of Douglas Hyde)

Fair Maidens' Beauty will Soon Fade Away

My love she was born in the North counterie.
Where the highlands of Antrim look over the sea;
My love is as fair as the soft smiling May;
But fair maidens' beauty will soon fade away.

My love is as pure as the bright blessèd well
That springs from Seefin in a green lonely dell;
My love she is graceful and tender and gay;
But fair maidens' beauty will soon fade away.

My love is as sweet as the cinnamon tree;
As the bark to its bough cleaves she firm unto me;
But the leaves they will wither and the roots will
    decay,
And fair maidens' beauty will soon fade away.

But love, though the green leaf may wither and fall,
Though the bright eye be dimmed, and the sweet
smile and all;
O, love has a life that shall never decay,
Though fair maidens' beauty will soon fade away.

Robert Dwyer Joyce

LV

Amoret

Fair Amoret is gone astray;
  Pursue and seek her, ev'ry lover;
I'll tell the signs by which you may
  The wandering shepherdess discover.

Coquet and coy at once her air,
  Both studied, though both seem neglected;
Careless she is with artful care,
  Affecting to seem unaffected.

With skill her eyes dart every glance,
  Yet change so soon you'd ne'er suspect them;
For she'd persuade they wound by chance,
  Though certain aim and art direct them.

She likes herself, yet others hates
  For that which in herself she prizes;
And, while she laughs at them, forgets
  She is the thing that she despises.

William Congreve

Bid Adieu, Adieu, Adieu

Bid adieu, adieu, adieu,
   Bid adieu to girlish days,
Happy Love is come to woo
   Thee and woo thy girlish ways—
The zone that doth become thee fair,
The snood upon thy yellow hair.

When thou hast heard his name upon
   The bugles of the cherubim
Begin thou softly to unzone
   Thy girlish bosom unto him
And softly to undo the snood
That is the sign of maidenhood.

James Joyce

June

Broom out the floor now, lay the fender by,
And plant this bee-sucked bough of woodbine
   there,
And let the window down. The butterfly

Floats in upon the sunbeam, and the fair
Tanned face of June, the nomad gipsy, laughs
Above her widespread wares, the while she tells
The farmers' fortunes in the fields, and quaffs
The water from the spider-peopled wells.

The hedges are all drowned in green grass seas,
And bobbing poppies flare like Elmor's light,
While siren-like the pollen-stainèd bees
Drone in the clover depths. And up the height
The cuckoo's voice is hoarse and broke with joy
And on the lowland crops the crows make raid,
Nor fear the clappers of the farmer's boy,
Who sleeps, like drunken Noah, in the shade.

And loop this red rose in that hazel ring
That snares your little ear, for June is short
And we must joy in it and dance and sing,
And from her bounty draw her rosy worth.
Ay! soon the swallows will be flying south,
The wind wheel north to gather in the snow,
Even the roses spilt on youth's red mouth
Will soon blow down the road all roses go.

Francis Ledwidge

Song

Ah, me! when shall I marry me?
  Lovers are plenty; but fail to relieve me.
He, fond youth, that could carry me,
  Offers to love, but means to deceive me.

But I will rally, and combat the ruiner:
  Not a look, not a smile shall my passion discover:
She that gives all to the false one pursuing her,
  Makes but a penitent, loses a lover.

                              Oliver Goldsmith

Dear Dark Head

Put your head, darling, darling, darling,
  Your darling black head my heart above;
Oh, mouth of honey, with the thyme for fragrance,
  Who, with heart in breast, could deny you love?

Oh, many and many a young girl for me is pining,
  Letting her locks of gold to the cold wind free,
For me, the foremost of our gay young fellows;
  But I'd leave a hundred, pure love, for thee!

Then put your head, darling, darling, darling,
  Your darling black head my heart above;
Oh, mouth of honey, with the thyme for fragrance,
  Who, with heart in breast, could deny you love?

Sir Samuel Ferguson
(From the Irish)

LX
At Mass

Ah! light, lovely lady with delicate lips aglow!
With breast more white than a branch heavy-laden
    with snow!
When my hand was lifted at Mass to salute the
    Host
I looked at you once and the half of my soul was
    lost.

Robin Flower
(From the Irish)

Perfection

By Perfection fooled too long,
I will dream of that no longer;
Venus, you have done me wrong
By your unattainable beauty,
Till it seemed to be my duty
To belittle all the throng.
I have found attraction stronger;
I have found a lady younger
Who can make a hard heart stir:
Like an athlete, tall and slender,
With no more than human splendour;
Yet, for all the faults of her,
Than Perfection perfecter.

Though she guards it, grace breaks through
Every blithe and careless movement;
What shall I compare her to?
When she takes the ball left-handed,
Speed and sweetness are so blended
Nothing awkward she can do,
She, whose faults are an improvement!
If she only knew what Love meant
I would not be seeking now

To describe the curved perfection
Of all loveliness in action—
Perfect she would be, I vow,
With the mole above the brow!

Oliver Gogarty

Stella's Birthday

All travellers at first incline
Where'er they see the fairest sign,
And if they find the chambers neat,
And like the liquor and the meat,
Will call again, and recommend
The Angel Inn to every friend.
And though the painting grows decay'd,
The house will never lose its trade:
Nay, though the treach'rous tapster, Thomas,
Hangs a new Angel two doors from us,
As fine as daubers' hands can make it,
In hopes that strangers may mistake it,
We think it both a shame and sin
To quit the true old Angel Inn.
    Now this is Stella's case in fact,
An angel's face a little crack'd.

(Could poets or could painters fix
How angels look at thirty-six:)
This drew us in at first to find
In such a form an angel's mind;
And every virtue now supplies
The fainting rays of Stella's eyes.
See, at her levee crowding swains,
Whom Stella freely entertains
With breeding, humour, wit, and sense,
And puts them to so small expense;
Their minds so plentifully fills,
And makes such reasonable bills,
So little gets for what she gives,
We really wonder how she lives!
And had her stock been less, no doubt
She must have long ago run out.

Then, who can think we'll quit the place,
When Doll hangs out a newer face?
Nail'd to her window full in sight
All Christian people to invite,
Or stop and light at Chloe's head,
With scraps and leavings to be fed?

Then, Chloe, still go on to prate
Of thirty-six and thirty-eight;
Pursue your trade of scandal-picking,
Your hints that Stella is no chicken;

Your innuendoes, when you tell us,
That Stella loves to talk with fellows:
But let me warn you to believe
A truth, for which your soul should grieve;
That should you live to see the day,
When Stella's locks must all be gray,
When age must print a furrow'd trace
On every feature of her face;
Though you, and all your senseless tribe,
Could Art, or Time, or Nature bribe,
To make you look like Beauty's Queen,
And hold for ever at fifteen;
No bloom of youth can ever blind
The cracks and wrinkles of your mind:
All men of sense will pass your door,
And crowd to Stella's at four-score.

Jonathan Swift

LXIII

The Lapful of Nuts

Whene'er I see soft hazel eyes
    And nut-brown curls,
I think of those bright days I spent
    Among the Limerick girls;

When up through Cratla woods I went,
　　Nutting with thee;
And we plucked the glossy clustering fruit
　　From many a bending tree.

Beneath the hazel boughs we sat,
　　Thou, love, and I,
And the gathered nuts lay in thy lap,
　　Beneath thy downcast eye:
But little we thought of the store we'd won,
　　I, love, or thou;
For our hearts were full, and we dare not own
　　The love that's spoken now.

Oh, there's wars for willing hearts in Spain,
　　And high Germanie!
And I'll come back, ere long, again,
　　With knightly fame and fee:
And I'll come back, if I ever come back,
　　Faithful to thee,
That sat with thy white lap full of nuts
　　Beneath the hazel tree.

Sir Samuel Ferguson
(From the Irish)

Echo

How sweet the answer Echo makes
    To music at night,
When, roused by lute or horn, she wakes,
And, far away, o'er lawns and lakes,
    Goes answering light.

Yet Love hath echoes truer far,
    And far more sweet,
Than e'er beneath the moonlight's star,
Or horn or lute, or soft guitar,
    The songs repeat.

'Tis when the sigh, in youth sincere,
    And only then,—
The sigh that's breathed for one to hear,
Is by that one, that only dear,
    Breathed back again!

Thomas Moore

The Poor Girl's Meditation

I am sitting here,
Since the moon rose in the night;
Kindling a fire,
And striving to keep it alight:
The folk of the house are lying
In slumber deep;
The cocks will be crowing soon:
The whole of the land is asleep.

May I never leave this world
Until my ill-luck is gone;
Till I have cows and sheep,
And the lad that I love for my own:
I would not think it long,
The night I would lie at his breast,
And the daughters of spite, after that,
Might say the thing they liked best.

Love covers up hate,
If a girl have beauty at all:
On a bed that was narrow and high,
A three-month I lie by the wall:
When I bethought on the lad

That I left on the brow of the hill,
I wept from dark until dark
And my cheeks have the tear-tracks still.

And, O, young lad that I love,
I am no mark for your scorn:
All you can say of me
Is undowered I was born:
And if I've no fortune in hand,
Nor cattle nor sheep of my own,
This I can say, O lad,
I am fitted to lie my lone!

Padraic Colum
(*From the Irish*)

LXVI

The Fairy Thorn

"Get up, our Anna dear, from the weary
    spinning-wheel;
  For your father's on the hill, and your mother is
    asleep:
Come up above the crags, and we'll dance a
    highland reel
  Around the fairy thorn on the steep."

At Anna Grace's door 'twas thus the maidens cried,
  Three merry maidens fair in kirtles of the green;
And Anna laid the rock and weary wheel aside,
  The fairest of the four, I ween.

They're glancing through the glimmer of the quiet
    eve,
  Away in milky wavings of neck and ankle bare;
The heavy-sliding stream in its sleepy song they
    leave,
  And the crags in the ghostly air:

And linking hand and hand, and singing as they go,
  The maids along the hill-side have ta'en their
    fearless way,
Till they come to where the rowan trees in lonely
    beauty grow
  Beside the Fairy Hawthorn grey.

The Hawthorn stands between the ashes tall and
    slim,
  Like matron with her twin grand-daughters at
    her knee;
The rowan berries cluster o'er her low head grey
    and dim
  In ruddy kisses sweet to see.

The merry maidens four have ranged them in
  a row,
  Between each lovely couple a stately rowan
  stem,
And away in mazes wavy, like skimming birds
  they go,
  Oh, never carolled bird like them!

But solemn is the silence of the silvery haze
  That drinks away their voices in echoless repose,
And dreamily the evening has stilled the haunted
  braes,
  And dreamier the gloaming grows.

And sinking one by one, like lark-notes from
  the sky
  When the falcon's shadow saileth across the
  open shaw,
Are hushed the maidens' voices, as cowering down
  they lie
  In the flutter of their sudden awe.

For, from the air above, and the grassy ground
  beneath,
  And from the mountain-ashes and the old
whitethorn between,

A Power of faint enchantment doth through their
    beings breathe,
  And they sink down together on the green.

They sink together silent, and stealing side to side,
  They fling their lovely arms o'er their drooping
    necks so fair,
They vainly strive again their naked arms to hide,
  For their shrinking necks again are bare.

Thus clasped and prostrate all, with their heads
    together bowed,
  Soft o'er their bosoms' beating—the only
  human sound—
They hear the silky footsteps of the silent fairy
    crowd,
  Like a river in the air, gliding round.

No scream can any raise, nor prayer can any say,
  But wild, wild, the terror of the speechless three—
For they feel fair Anna Grace drawn silently away,
  By whom they dare not look to see.

They feel their tresses twine with her parting locks
of gold,
  And the curls elastic falling, as her head
withdraws;

They feel her sliding arms from their tranced arms
        unfold,
    But they may not look to see the cause:

For heavy on their senses the faint enchantment
        lies
    Through all that night of anguish and perilous
        amaze;
And neither fear nor wonder can ope their
        quivering eyes
    Or their limbs from the cold ground raise,

Till out of night the earth has rolled her dewy side,
    With every haunted mountain and streamy vale
        below;
When, as the mist dissolves in the yellow morning
        tide,
    The maidens' trance dissolveth so.

Then fly the ghastly three as swiftly as they may,
    And tell their tale of sorrow to anxious friends
        in vain—
They pined away and died within the year and
        day,
    And ne'er was Anna Grace seen again.

                                    Sir Samuel Ferguson

A Bud in the Frost

Blow on the embers, an' sigh at the sparkles!
My mother she bid me be wise in time.—
Ashes are white an' the red fire darkles;
I lost the words, but I know the rhyme.
It may be true,
An' it may be true,
'Tis much to me, 'tis little to you!
Oh, look if a boat comes over the water,
An' call on my mother who told her daughter
That "Love is all crost,—like a bud in the frost."

Love has undone me, an' why would you wonder!
My mother she bid me be wise in time.—
The waters have met, an' my head has gone under,
But far, far away there are bells that chime
How love is no liar,
Oh, love is no liar.
"That's only a bird singin' there on the briar.
You'd better be lookin' no more at the water,
But give me your hand an' come home, my
daughter,
For love is all crost,—like a bud in the frost."

Moira O'Neill

Do You Remember that Night?

Do you remember that night
When you were at the window,
With neither hat nor gloves
Nor coat to shelter you?
I reached out my hand to you,
And you ardently grasped it;
I remained to converse with you
Until the lark began to sing.

Do you remember that night
That you and I were
At the foot of the rowan-tree,
And the night drifting snow?
Your head on my breast,
And your pipe sweetly playing?
Little thought I that night
That our love ties would loosen!

Beloved of my inmost heart,
Come some night, and soon,
When my people are at rest,
That we may talk together.
My arms shall encircle you
While I relate my sad tale,

That your soft, pleasant converse
Hath deprived me of heaven.

The fire is unraked,
The light unextinguished,
The key under the door,
Do you softly draw it.
My mother is asleep,
But I am wide awake;
My fortune in my hand,
I am ready to go with you.

George Petrie
(From the Irish)

LXIX
Shule Aroon

I would I were on yonder hill,
'Tis there I'd sit and cry my fill,
And every tear would turn a mill,
Is go d-teidh tu, a mburnin, slan!
  Siubhail, siubhail, siubhail, a ruin!
  Siubhail go socair, agus siubhail go ciuin,
  Siubhail go d-ti an doras agus eulaigh liom,
  Is go d-teidh tu, a mburnin, slan!

I'll sell my rock, I'll sell my reel,
I'll sell my only spinning-wheel,
To buy for my love a sword of steel,
Is go d-teidh, a mburnin, slan!
    Siubhail, siubhail, siubhail, a ruin! etc.

I'll dye my petticoats, I'll dye them red,
And round the world I'll beg my bread,
Until my parents shall wish me dead,
Is go d-teidh, a mburnin, slan!
    Siubhail, siubhail, siubhail, a ruin! etc.

I wish, I wish, I wish in vain,
I wish I had my heart again,
And vainly think I'd not complain,
Is go d-teidh, a mburnin, slan!
    Siubhail, siubhail, siubhail, a ruin! etc.

But now my love has gone to France,
To try his fortune to advance;
If he e'er come back, 'tis but a chance,
Is go d-teidh, a mburnin, slan!
    Siubhail, siubhail, siubhail, a ruin! etc.

Anonymous
(From the Irish)

LXX

My Love, Oh, She is My Love

My love, oh, she is my love,
  The woman who is most for destroying me;
  Dearer is she from making me ill
  Than the woman who would be for making
    me well.

She is my treasure, oh, she is my treasure,
  The woman of the grey eye, she like the rose,
  A woman who would not place a hand beneath
    my head,
  A woman who would not be with me for gold.

She is my affection, oh, she is my affection,
  The woman who left no strength in me;
  A woman who would not breathe a sigh after me,
  A woman who would not raise a stone at my
    tomb.

She is my secret love, oh, she is my secret love,
  A woman who tells me nothing;
  A woman who would not breathe a sigh after me,
  A woman who would not shed tears.

It is she ruined my heart,
    And left a sigh for ever in me.
    Unless this evil be raised off my heart,
    I shall not be well for ever.

Douglas Hyde
(From the Irish)

LXXI

I Hear an Army Charging

I hear an army charging upon the land,
    And the thunder of horses plunging, foam about
        their knees:
Arrogant, in black armour, behind them stand,
    Disdaining the reins, with fluttering whips, the
        charioteers.

They cry unto the night their battle-name:
    I moan in sleep when I hear afar their whirling
        laughter.
They cleave the gloom of dreams, a blinding flame,
    Clanging, clanging upon the heart as upon an
        anvil.

They come shaking in triumph their long, green
   hair:
   They come out of the sea and run shouting by
      the shore.
My heart, have you no wisdom thus to despair?
   My love, my love, my love, why have you left
      me alone?

James Joyce

LXXII
Haunted

At the wayside well I stooped down for to drink,
But the thirst was on me yet when I left the brink;
For I would not put my lips to the water cool
While the face of a dead young girl looked out o'
   the pool.

By the high moor-road I stopped to rest awhile,
For I had travelled many a heavy mile;
But I rose up from the heather spent an' weak,
For the hand of a dead young girl had touched my
   cheek.

An' once, where three roads met, I stopped to hear
A fiddlin' fellow makin' music clear,

But I wandered on before his tune was done,
For the voice of a dead young girl in the song
    made moan.

So on an' on I go, and have no rest
To ease the hungry sorrow of my breast;
And always at my side I hear the tread,
The swift light footsteps of a young girl dead.

Helen Lanyon

LXXIII
And Then No More

I saw her once, one little while, and then no more:
'Twas Eden's light on Earth awhile, and then no
    more.
Amid the throng she passed along the
    meadow-floor:
Spring seemed to smile on Earth awhile, and then
    no more;
But whence she came, which way she went, what
    garb she wore
I noted not; I gazed awhile, and then no more!

I saw her once, one little while, and then no more:
'Twas Paradise on Earth awhile, and then no more.

Ah! what avail my vigils pale, my magic lore?
She shone before mine eyes awhile, and then no
    more.
The shallop of my peace is wrecked on Beauty's
    shore.
Near Hope's fair isle it rode awhile, and then no
    more!

I saw her once, one little while, and then no more:
The earth was Peri-land awhile, and then no more.
Oh, might I see but once again, as once before,
Through chance or wile, that shape awhile, and
    then no more!
Death soon would heal my griefs! This heart, now
    sad and sore,
Would beat anew a little while, and then no more.

James Clarence Mangan

The Song of Wandering Aengus

I went out to the hazel wood,
Because a fire was in my head.
And cut and peeled a hazel wand,
And hooked a berry to a thread;

And when white moths were on the wing,
And moth-like stars were flickering out,
I dropped the berry in a stream
And caught a little silver trout.

When I had laid it on the floor
I went to blow the fire a-flame,
But something rustled on the floor,
And some one called me by my name:
It had become a glimmering girl
With apple blossom in her hair
Who called me by my name and ran
And faded through the brightening air.

Though I am old with wandering
Through hollow lands and hilly lands,
I will find out where she has gone,
And kiss her lips and take her hands;
And walk among long dappled grass,
And pluck till time and times are done
The silver apples of the moon,
The golden apples of the sun.

W. B. Yeats

Cashel of Munster

I'd wed you without herds, without money, or rich
  array,
And I'd wed you on a dewy morning at day-dawn
  grey;
My bitter woe it is, love, that we are not far away
In Cashel town, though the bare deal board were
  our marriage-bed this day!

Oh, fair maid, remember the green hill side,
Remember how I hunted about the valleys wide;
Time now has worn me; my locks are turned to
  grey,
The year is scarce and I am poor, but send me
  not, love, away!

Oh, deem not my blood is of base strain, my girl,
Oh, deem not my birth was as the birth of the
  churl;
Marry me, and prove me, and say soon you will,
That noble blood is written on my right side still!

My purse holds no red gold, no coin of the silver
  white,

No herds are mine to drive through the long
  twilight!
But the pretty girl that would take me, all bare
  though I be and lone,
Oh, I'd take her with me kindly to the county
  Tyrone.

Oh, my girl, I can see 'tis in trouble you are,
And, oh, my girl, I see 'tis your people's reproach
  you bear:
"I am a girl in trouble for his sake with whom I fly,
And, oh, may no other maiden know such
  reproach as I!"

Sir Samuel Ferguson
(From the Irish)

LXXVI

Love's Despair

I am desolate,
  Bereft by bitter fate;
No cure beneath the skies can save me,
  No cure on sea or strand,
  Nor in any human hand—
But hers, this paining wound who gave me.

I know not night from day,
      Nor thrush from cuckoo gray,
Nor cloud from the sun that shines above thee—
      Nor freezing cold from heat,
      Nor friend—if friend I meet—
I but know—heart's love!—I love thee.

      Love that my Life began,
      Love, that will close life's span,
Love that grows ever by love-giving:
      Love, from the first to last,
      Love, till all life be passed,
Love that loves on after living!

      This love I gave to thee,
      For pain love has given me,
Love that can fail or falter never—
      But, spite of earth above,
      Guards thee, my Flower of love,
Thou marvel-maid of life for ever.

      Bear all things evidence,
      Thou art my very sense,
My past, my present, and my morrow!
      All else on earth is crossed,
      All in the world is lost—
Lost all—but the great love-gift of sorrow.

My life not life, but death;
My voice not voice—a breath;
No sleep, no quiet—thinking ever
On thy fair phantom face,
Queen eyes and royal grace,
Lost loveliness that leaves me never.

I pray thee grant but this—
From thy dear mouth one kiss,
That the pang of death-despair pass over:
Or bid make ready nigh
The place where I shall lie,
For aye, thy leal and silent lover.

George Sigerson
(From the Irish of Dermot O'Curnan)

LXXVII

When the Ecstatic Body Grips

When the ecstatic body grips
Its heaven, with little sobbing cries,
And lips are crushed on hot blind lips,
I read strange pity in your eyes.

For that in you which is not mine,
And that in you which I love best,

And that, which my day-thoughts divine
Masterless still, still unpossessed,

Sits in the blue eyes' frightened stare,
A naked lonely-dwelling thing,
A frail thing from its body-lair
Drawn at my body's summoning;

Whispering low, "O unknown man,
Whose hunger on my hunger wrought,
Body shall give what body can,
Shall give you all—save what you sought."

Whispering, "O secret one, forgive,
Forgive and be content though still
Beyond the blood's surrender live
The darkness of the separate will.

"Enough if in the veins we know
Body's delirium, body's peace—
Ask not that ghost to ghost shall go,
Essence in essence merge and cease."

But swiftly, as in sudden sleep,
That You in you is veiled or dead;
And the world's shrunken to a heap
Of hot flesh straining on a bed.

E. R. Dodds

A Deep-Sworn Vow

Others because you did not keep
That deep-sworn vow have been friends of mine;
Yet always when I look death in the face,
When I clamber to the heights of sleep,
Or when I grow excited with wine,
Suddenly I meet your face.

W. B. Yeats

The Troubled Friar

Friends, are ye sad for the troubled Friar,
   Scorched by desire and blight of soul,
Roaming through valleys and lonesome mountains,
   While all his heart is a kindled coal.

His ears are shrunk to his rounded shoulders,
   And death has called him with one loud call,
And not a man who has known his story
   But says "Alas! for the Bráthair Bán."

Saw ye her passing, the swan so slender,
    Graceful and tender and queenly bright,
Alas! the day that her mother bore her,
    Fate set before her my death and blight.

What were, without her, the whole world's riches;
    When she bewitches, I all forget.
You are killing me, love, with your love. I met you.
    I tried to get you. I could not get.

On no wild mountain, but in a valley
    Fruitful and happy, my love shines bright,
Where trout are leaping and calves are lowing,
    And red wheat growing, and barley white.

Where the rush drops honey, the cream makes
        butter,
    And no cold comes from the skies above.
Had I been prudent I might be in it
    And pouring honey for her I love.

Oh! false and cruel the things they told her,
    That where I rove no grass will grow;
That the moon keeps back her borrowed light
    And the stars of the night refuse to glow!

But till the seasons are passed for ever,
   Till sea and river are all gone dry,
Till the onset of ocean the rocks shall sever
   This heart shall never its love deny.

Douglas Hyde
(From the Irish)

LXXX
Deirdre

Do not let any woman read this verse;
It is for men, and after them their sons
And their sons' sons.

The time comes when our hearts sink utterly;
When we remember Deirdre and her tale,
And that her lips are dust.

Once she did tread the earth; men took her hand;
They looked into her eyes and said their say,
And she replied to them.

More than a thousand years it is since she
Was beautiful; she trod the waving grass;
She saw the clouds.

A thousand years! The grass is still the same,
The clouds as lovely as they were that time
When Deirdre was alive.

But there has never been a woman born
Who was so beautiful, not one so beautiful
Of all the women born.

Let all men go apart and mourn together;
No man can ever love her; not a man
Can ever be her lover.

No man can bend before her; no man say—
What could one say to her? There are no words
That one could say to her!

Now she is but a story that is told
Beside the fire! No man can ever be
The friend of that poor queen.

James Stephens

LXXXI

O Love, There is No Beauty

O love, there is no beauty,
No sorrowful beauty, but I have seen;
There is no island that has gathered sound

117

Into dim stone from many reeded waters
But we have known.

                    Heart of my sorrowful heart,
Beauty fades out from sleepy pool to pool
And there is a crying of wings about me
And a crying in me lest I lose you. Glimmer
Around me; sound, O weir, within my heart;
Bring calm on many waters, for I will be hearing
The salmon shatter the air into silver when
The chill grass ends their leaping.

                              As I was dreaming
Between the pines, she gleamed from windy heights
Pale-browed, in a dark battlemented storm
Of hair. Far down I wander in the woods,
Ankle-deep in autumn, who am light
And lost of the waters.

                         I have no clan but her;
Being a dream, though the fierce incense burn,
Love, love me, as no woman ever loved
With intellect tense and more passionate
Than the heart, for when the hunger of ourselves
Is over, there is no joy but in the mind.
Think in me for I am become as water
Under the mountain-minds, and when the fire
Of intellect has taken me their minds

Reflect as thought reveals myself. Therefore,
My days are smoke and westward praise of god.
When I eat bread I choke with the fierce salt
Of dream. Therefore I have lived for the sun,
And looked from every cape, and I have been
A runner on swift feet that I might break
The tapes of life.

                 Drag down your lonely hair
On breasts no child has ever known, for it
Will bring you happy sleep and peace. There is
No peace within my words. I will be secret
Lest the loud powers that move in wine and satire
Gathering themselves from me, the lonely gate
And fire, perplex you with the ancient storm
No woman can endure.

                     But O there was
No knowing her sad beauty that was made
For candlelight and sleep. Yet thinking I
Forgo her, though she has left me bare; I sing
And the mountain hawk is sinking slower through
    glens
Of lonely air.

                              I know the steps of love
Take hands with me, sad dancers in the glen,
For autumn leaves dance best when they are dead
And we are less than them, O bitter dancers
That dance with bloody feet.

Austin Clarke

Come, Let us Make Love Deathless

Come, let us make love deathless, thou and I,
    Seeing that our footing on the Earth is brief—
Seeing that her multitudes sweep out to die
    Mocking at all that passes their belief.
For standard of our love not theirs we take;
        If we go hence to-day
Fill the high cup that is so soon to break
With richer wine than they!

Ay, since beyond these walls no heavens there be
    Joy to revive or wasted youth repair,
I'll not bedim the lovely flame in thee
    Nor sully the sad splendour that we wear.

Great be thy love, if with the lover dies
    Our greatness past recall,
And nobler for the fading of those eyes
    The world seen once for all!

Herbert Trench

LXXXIII
To the Oaks of Glencree

My arms are round you, and I lean
Against you, while the lark
Sings over us, and golden lights, and green
Shadows are on your bark.

There'll come a season when you'll stretch
Black boards to cover me:
Then in Mount Jerome I will lie, poor wretch,
With worms eternally.

J. M. Synge

A Question

I asked if I got sick and died, would you
With my black funeral go walking too,
If you'd stand close to hear them talk or pray
While I'm let down in that steep bank of clay.

And, No, you said, for if you saw a crew
Of living idiots pressing round that new
Oak coffin—they alive, I dead beneath
That board—you'd rave and rend them with your
    teeth.

J. M. Synge

Last Night

I sat with one I love last night,
   She sang to me an olden strain;
In former times it woke delight.
      Last night—but pain.

Last night we saw the stars arise,
  But clouds soon dimm'd the ether blue:
And when we sought each other's eyes
    Tears dimm'd them too!

We paced alone our fav'rite walk
  But paced in silence broken-hearted:
Of old we used to smile and talk.
    Last night—we parted.

George Darley

LXXXVI

She Comes not When Noon is on the Roses

She comes not when Noon is on the roses—
    Too bright is Day.
She comes not to the Soul till it reposes
    From work and play.

But when Night is on the hills, and the great
    Voices
    Roll in from sea,
By starlight and by candlelight and dreamlight
    She comes to me.

Herbert Trench

The Priests and the Friars

The priests and the friars are every day in anger
    with me
For my being in love with thee, O maiden, and
    thou dead.
I would protect thee from the wind and shelter
    thee from the rain,
And the bitter melancholy of my heart it is, thee
    to be down within the ground.

When my people are certain that I am lying on
    my bed,
It is on thy tomb that I do be stretched from
    nightfall to morning.
Brooding upon my hardship, and bitterly
    lamenting and sorely,
For my gentle courteous girl who was betrothed to
    me when a child.

Dost thou remember the night that I and thou
    were at the foot of the blackthorn tree,
And the night freezing hard?
A thousand thanks to Jesus that we made not the
    spoiling,

And thy crown of maidenhood is now like a shaft
    of light shining before thee.

Douglas Hyde
(From the Irish)

LXXXVIII
Donall Oge

It is late last night the dog was speaking of you,
The snipe was speaking of you in her deep marsh.
It is you are the lonely bird throughout the woods,
And that you may be without a mate until you
    find me.

You promised me and you said a lie to me,
That you would be before me where the sheep are
    flocked.
I gave a whistle and three hundred cries to you,
And I found nothing there but a bleating lamb.

You promised me a thing that was hard for you,
A ship of gold under a silver mast,
Twelve towns and a market in all of them,
And a fine white court by the side of the sea.

You promised me a thing that is not possible,
That you would give me gloves of the skin of a
  fish,
That you would give me shoes of the skin of a
  bird,
And a suit of the dearest silk in Ireland.

My mother said to me not to be talking with you,
To-day or to-morrow or on the Sunday.
It was a bad time she took for telling me that,
It was shutting the door after the house was
  robbed.

You have taken the east from me, you have taken
  the west from me,
You have taken what is before me and what is
  behind me;
You have taken the moon, you have taken the sun
  from me,
And my fear is great you have taken God
  from me.

Lady Gregory
(From the Irish)

The Red Man's Wife

'Tis what they say,
  Thy little heel fits in a shoe.
'Tis what they say,
  Thy little mouth kisses well, too.
'Tis what they say,
  Thousand loves that you leave me to rue;
That the tailor went the way
  That the wife of the Red man knew.

Nine months did I spend
  In a prison closed tightly and bound;
Bolts on my smalls
  And a thousand locks frowning around;
But o'er the tide
  I would leap with the leap of a swan,
Could I once set my side
  By the bride of the Red-haired man.

I thought, O my life,
  That one house between us love would be;
And I thought I would find
  You once coaxing my child on your knee:
But now the curse of the High One

On him let it be,
And on all of the band of the liars
    Who put silence between you and me.

There grows a tree in the garden
    With blossoms that tremble and shake,
I lay my hand on its bark
    And I feel that my heart must break.
On one wish alone
    My soul through the long months ran,
One little kiss
    From the wife of the Red-haired man.

But the Day of Doom shall come,
    And hills and harbours be rent;
A mist shall fall on the sun
    From the dark clouds heavily sent;
The sea shall be dry,
    And earth under mourning and ban;
Then loud shall he cry
    For the wife of the Red-haired man.

Douglas Hyde
(From the Irish)

The Enchanted Mistress

I met brightness of brightness upon the path of
    loneliness;
Plaiting of plaiting in every lock of her yellow hair.
News of news she gave me, and she as lonely as
    she was;
News of the coming back of him that owns the
    tribute of the king.

Folly of follies I to go so near to her,
Slave I was made by a slave that put me in hard
    bonds.
She made away from me then and I following
    after her
Till we came to a house of houses made by Druid
    enchantments.

They broke into mocking laughter, a troop of men
    of enchantments,
And a troop of young girls with smooth-plaited
    hair.
They put me up in chains, they made no delay
    about it—
And my love holding to her breast an awkward
    ugly clown.

I told her then with the truest words I could tell
    her,
It was not right for her to be joined with a
    common clumsy churl;
And the man that was three times fairer than the
    whole race of the Scots
Waiting till she would come to him to be his
    beautiful bride.

At the sound of my words her pride set her
    crying,
The tears were running down over the kindling of
    her cheeks.
She sent a lad to bring me safe from the place I
    was in.
She is the brightness of brightness I met in the
    path of loneliness.

Lady Gregory
(From the Irish of Egan O'Rahilly)

I Shall not Die for Thee

For thee I shall not die,
    Woman high of fame and name;
Foolish men thou mayest slay,
    I and they are not the same.

Why should I expire
    For the fire of any eye,
Slender waist or swan-like limb,
    Is't for them that I should die?

The round breasts, the fresh skin,
    Cheeks crimson, hair so long and rich;
Indeed, indeed, I shall not die,
    Please God, not I, for any such.

The golden hair, the forehead thin,
    The chaste mien, the gracious ease,
The rounded heel, the languid tone,
    Fools alone find death from these.

Thy sharp wit, thy perfect calm,
    Thy thin palm like foam of sea;
Thy white neck, thy blue eye,
    I shall not die for thee.

Woman, graceful as the swan,
  A wise man did nurture me,
Little palm, white neck, bright eye,
  I shall not die for thee.

Douglas Hyde
(From the Irish)

XCII

The Man Who Trod on Sleeping Grass

In a field by Cahirconlish
  I trod on sleeping grass,
No cry I made to heaven
  From my dumb lips would pass.

Three days, three nights I slumbered,
  And till I woke again
Those I have loved have sought me,
  And sorrowed all in vain.

My neighbours still upbraid me,
  And murmur as I pass,
"There goes a man enchanted,
  He trod on fairy grass."

My little ones around me,
  They claim my old caress,
I push them roughly from me
  With hands that cannot bless.

My wife upon my shoulder
  A bitter tear lets fall,
I turn away in anger
  And love her not at all.

For like a man surrounded,
  In some sun-haunted lane,
By countless wings that follow,
  A grey and stinging chain,

Around my head for ever
  I hear small voices speak
In tongues I cannot follow,
  I know not what they seek.

I raise my hands to find them
  When autumn winds go by,
And see between my fingers
  A broken summer fly.

I raise my hands to hold them
    When winter days are near,
And clasp a falling snowflake
    That breaks into a tear.

And ever follows laughter
    That echoes through my heart,
From some delights forgotten
    Where once I had a part.

What love comes half-remembered,
    In half-forgotten bliss?
Who lay upon my bosom,
    And had no human kiss?

Where is the land I loved in?
    What music did I sing
That left my ears enchanted
    Inside the fairy ring?

I see my neighbours shudder,
    And whisper as I pass:
"Three nights the fairies stole him;
    He trod on sleeping grass."

Dora Sigerson Shorter

The Outlaw of Lough Lene

Oh, many a day have I made good ale in the glen,
That came not of stream or malt—like the
    brewing of men.
My bed was the ground; my roof, the greenwood
    above,
And the wealth that I sought, one far kind glance
    from my love.

Alas! on that night when the horses I drove from
    the field,
That I was not near from terror my angel to shield.
She stretched forth her arms—her mantle she
    flung to the wind,
And swam o'er Loch Lene her outlawed lover to
    find.

Oh, would that a freezing, sleet-winged tempest
    did sweep,
And I and my love were alone, far off on the deep!
I'd ask not a ship, or a bark, or a pinnace, to save,—
With her hand round my waist I'd fear not the
    wind or the wave.

'Tis down by the lake where the wild-tree fringes
    its sides
The maid of my heart, my fair one of Heaven
    resides;
I think as at eve she wanders its mazes along,
The birds go to sleep by the sweet, wild twist of
    her song.

Jeremiah Joseph Callanan
(From the Irish)

XCIV

Aghadoe

There's a glade in Aghadoe, Aghadoe, Aghadoe,
There's a green and silent glade in Aghadoe,
    Where we met, my Love and I, Love's fair
        planet in the sky,
O'er that sweet and silent glade in Aghadoe.

There's a glen in Aghadoe, Aghadoe, Aghadoe,
There's a deep and secret glen in Aghadoe,
    Where I hid him from the eyes of the redcoats
        and their spies
That year the trouble came to Aghadoe!

Oh! my curse on one black heart in Aghadoe,
　　Aghadoe,
On Shaun Dhuv, my mother's son in Aghadoe,
　When your throat fries in hell's drouth salt the
　　flame be in your mouth,
For the treachery you did in Aghadoe!

For they tracked me to that glen in Aghadoe,
　　Aghadoe,
When the price was on his head in Aghadoe;
　O'er the mountain through the wood, as I stole
　　to him with food,
When in hiding lone he lay in Aghadoe.

But they never took him living in Aghadoe,
　　Aghadoe;
With the bullets in his heart in Aghadoe,
　There he lay, the head—my breast keeps the
　　warmth where once 'twould rest—
Gone, to win the traitor's gold from Aghadoe!

I walked to Mallow Town from Aghadoe, Aghadoe,
Brought his head from the gaol's gate to Aghadoe,
　Then I covered him with fern, and I piled on
　　him the cairn,
Like an Irish king he sleeps in Aghadoe.

Oh, to creep into that cairn in Aghadoe, Aghadoe!
There to rest upon his breast in Aghadoe!
  Sure your dog for you could die with no truer
      heart than I—
Your own love cold on your cairn in Aghadoe.

John Todhunter

XCV

Deirdre's Lament for the Sons of Usnach

> The lions of the hill are gone,
> And I am left alone—alone—
> Dig the grave both wide and deep,
> For I am sick, and fain would sleep!
>
> The falcons of the wood are flown,
> And I am left alone—alone—
> Dig the grave both deep and wide,
> And let us slumber side by side.
>
> The dragons of the rock are sleeping,
> Sleep that wakes not for our weeping:
> Dig the grave and make it ready;
> Lay me on my true Love's body.

Lay their spears and bucklers bright
By the warriors' sides aright;
Many a day the Three before me
On their linkèd bucklers bore me.

Lay upon the low grave floor,
'Neath each head, the blue claymore;
Many a time the noble Three
Redden'd those blue blades for me.

Lay the collars, as is meet,
Of their greyhounds at their feet;
Many a time for me have they
Brought the tall red deer to bay.

Oh! to hear my true Love singing,
Sweet as sound of trumpets ringing:
Like the sway of ocean swelling
Roll'd his deep voice round our dwelling

Oh! to hear the echoes pealing,
Round our green and fairy sheeling,
When the Three, with soaring chorus,
Pass'd the silent skylark o'er us.

Echo now, sleep, morn and even—
Lark alone enchant the heaven!—
Ardan's lips are scant of breath,—
Neesa's tongue is cold in death.

Stag, exult on glen and mountain—
Salmon, leap from loch to fountain—
Heron, in the free air warm ye—
Usnach's Sons no more will harm ye!

Erin's stay no more you are,
Rulers of the ridge of war;
Never more 'twill be your fate
To keep the beam of battle straight.

Woe is me! by fraud and wrong—
Traitors false and tyrants strong—
Fell Clan Usnach, bought and sold,
For Barach's feast and Conor's gold!

Woe to Eman, roof and wall!—
Woe to Red Branch, hearth and hall!—
Tenfold woe and black dishonour
To the false and foul Clan Conor!

Dig the grave both wide and deep,
Sick I am, and fain would sleep!
Dig the grave and make it ready,
Lay me on my true Love's body.

Sir Samuel Ferguson
(From the Irish)

XCVI

The Stag

An old man said, "I saw
The chief of the things that are gone;
A stag with head held high,
A doe, and a fawn;

"And they were the deer of Ireland
That scorned to breed within bound:
The last; they left no race
Tame on a pleasure ground.

"A stag, with his hide all rough
With the dew, and a doe and a fawn;
Nearby, on their track on the mountain
I watched them, two and one,

"Down to the Shannon going—
Did its waters cease to flow,
When they passed, they that carried the swiftness,
And the pride of long ago?

"The last of the troop that had heard
Finn's and Oscar's cry;
A doe and a fawn, and before
A stag with head held high!"

Padraic Colum

The Harp That Once Through
Tara's Halls

The harp that once through Tara's halls
  The soul of music shed,
Now hangs as mute on Tara's walls
  As if that soul were fled.
So sleeps the pride of former days,
  So glory's thrill is o'er,
And hearts, that once beat high for praise,
  Now feel that pulse no more.
No more to chiefs and ladies bright
  The harp of Tara swells;

The chord alone, that breaks at night,
    Its tale of ruin tells.
Thus freedom now so seldom wakes,
    The only throb she gives,
Is when some heart indignant breaks,
    To show that still she lives.

Thomas Moore

XCVIII
Kincora

Oh, where, Kincora! is Brian the Great?
And where is the beauty that once was thine?
Oh, where are the princes and nobles that sate
At the feast in thy halls, and drank the red wine?
      Where, oh, Kincora?

Oh, where, Kincora! are thy valorous lords?
Oh, whither, thou Hospitable! are they gone?
Oh, where are the Dalcassians of the Golden
    Swords?
And where are the warriors Brian led on?
      Where, oh, Kincora?

And where is Murrough, the descendant of kings—
The defeater of a hundred—the daringly brave—
Who set but slight store by jewels and rings—
Who swam down the torrent and laughed at its
    wave?
            Where, oh, Kincora?

And where is Donogh, King Brian's worthy son?
And where is Conaing, the Beautiful Chief?
And Kian, and Core? Alas! they are gone—
They have left me this night alone with my grief,
            Left me, Kincora!

And where are the chiefs with whom Brian went
    forth,
The ne'er vanquished son of Evin the Brave,
The great King of Onaght, renowned for his worth,
And the hosts of Baskinn, from the western wave?
            Where, oh, Kincora?

Oh, where is Duvlann of the Swift-footed Steeds?
And where is Kian, who was son of Molloy?
And where is King Lonergan, the fame of whose
    deeds
In the red battle-field no time can destroy?
            Where, oh, Kincora?

And where is that youth of majestic height,
The faith-keeping Prince of the Scots?—Even he,
As wide as his fame was, as great as was his might,
Was tributary, oh, Kincora, to thee!
        Thee, oh, Kincora!

They are gone, those heroes of royal birth
Who plundered no churches, and broke no trust,
'Tis weary for me to be living on earth
When they, oh, Kincora, lie low in the dust!
        Low, oh, Kincora!

Oh, never again will Princes appear,
To rival the Dalcassians of the Cleaving Swords!
I can never dream of meeting afar or anear,
In the east or the west, such heroes and lords!
        Never, Kincora!

Oh, dear are the images my memory calls up
Of Brian Boru!—how he never would miss
To give me at the banquet the first bright cup!
Ah! why did he heap on me honour like this?
        Why, oh, Kincora?

I am Mac Liag, and my home is on the Lake;
Thither often, to that palace whose beauty is fled,
Came Brian to ask me, and I went for his sake.
Oh, my grief! that I should live, and Brian be dead!
     Dead, oh, Kincora!

James Clarence Mangan
(From the Irish)

XCIX

The Woman of Beare

Ebbing, the wave of the sea
Leaves, where it wantoned before,
Wan and naked the shore,
Heavy the clotted weed.
And in my heart, woe is me!
Ebbs a wave of the sea.

I am the Woman of Beare.
Foul am I that was fair,
Gold-embroidered smocks I had,
Now in rags am hardly clad.

Arms, now so poor and thin,
Staring bone and shrunken skin,

Once were lustrous, once caressed
Chiefs and warriors to their rest.

Not the sage's power, nor lone
Splendour of an agèd throne,
Wealth I envy not, nor state.
Only women folk I hate.

On your heads, while I am cold,
Shines the sun of living gold.
Flowers shall wreathe your necks in May:
For me, every month is grey.

Yours the bloom: but ours the fire,
Even out of dead desire.
Wealth, not men, ye love; but when
Life was in us, we loved men.

Fair the men, and wild the manes
Of their coursers on the plains;
Wild the chariots rocked, when we
Raced by them for mastery.

Lone is Femen: vacant, bare,
Stands in Bregon Ronan's Chair.
And the slow tooth of the sky
Frets the stones where my dead lie.

The wave of the great sea talks:
Through the forest winter walks.
Not to-day by wood and sea
Comes King Diarmuid here to me.

I know what my king does.
Through the shivering reeds, across
Fords no mortal strength may breast,
He rows—to how chill a rest!

Amen! Time ends all.
Every acorn has to fall.
Bright at feasts the candles were,
Dark is here the house of prayer.

I, that when the hour was mine
Drank with kings the mead and wine,
Drink whey-water now, in rags
Praying among shrivelled hags.

Amen! Let my drink be whey,
Let me do God's will all day—
And, as upon God I call,
Turn my blood to angry gall.

Ebb, flood, and ebb: I know
Well the ebb, and well the flow,

And the second ebb, all three—
Have they not come home to me?

Came the flood that had for waves
Monarchs, mad to be my slaves,
Crested as by foam with bounds
Of wild steeds and leaping hounds.

Comes no more that flooding tide
To my silent dark fireside.
Guests are many in my hall,
But a hand has touched them all.

Well is with the isle that feels
Now the ocean backward steals:
But to me my ebbing blood
Brings again no forward flood.

Ebbing, the wave of the sea
Leaves, where it wantoned before,
Changed past knowing the shore,
Lean and lonely and grey.
And far and farther from me
Ebbs the wave of the sea.

Stephen Gwynn
(From the Irish)

Clann Cartie

My heart is withered and my health is gone,
For they who were not easy put upon,
Masters of mirth and of fair clemency,
Masters of wealth and gentle charity,
They are all gone. Mac Caura Mór is dead,
Mac Caura of the Lee is finishèd,
Mac Caura of Kanturk joined clay to clay
And gat him gone, and bides as deep as they.

Their years, their gentle deeds, their flags are
    furled,
And deeply down, under the stiffened world,
In chests of oaken wood are princes thrust,
To crumble day by day into the dust
A mouth might puff at; nor is left a trace
Of those who did of grace all that was grace.

O Wave of Cliona, cease thy bellowing!
And let mine ears forget a while to ring
At thy long, lamentable misery:
The great are dead indeed, the great are dead;
And I, in little time, will stoop my head
And put it under, and will be forgot
With them, and be with them, and thus be not:

Ease thee, cease thy long keening, cry no more:
End is, and here is end, and end is sore,
And to all lamentation be there end:
If I might come on thee, O howling friend!
Knowing that sails were drumming on the sea
Westward to Eiré, and that help would be
Trampling for her upon a Spanish deck,
I'd ram thy lamentation down thy neck.

James Stephens
(*From the Irish of Egan O'Rahilly*)

CI
Dirge of the Munster Forest
1591

Bring out the hemlock! bring the funeral yew!
The faithful ivy that doth all enfold;
Heap high the rocks, the patient brown earth strew,
And cover them against the numbing cold.
Marshal my retinue of bird and beast,
Wren, titmouse, robin, birds of every hue;
Let none keep back, no, not the very least,
Nor fox, nor deer, nor tiny nibbling crew,
Only bid one of all my forest clan
Keep far from us on this our funeral day.

On the grey wolf I lay my sovereign ban,
The great grey wolf who scrapes the earth away;
Lest, with hooked claw and furious hunger, he
Lay bare my dead for gloating foes to see—
Lay bare my dead, who died, and died for me.

For I must surely die as they have died,
And lo! my doom stands yoked and linked with
    theirs;
The axe is sharpened to cut down my pride:
I pass, I die, and leave no natural heirs.
Soon shall my sylvan coronals be cast;
My hidden sanctuaries, my secret ways,
Naked must stand to the rebellious blast;
No Spring shall quicken what this Autumn slays.

Therefore, while still I keep my russet crown,
I summon all my lieges to the feast.
Hither, ye flutterers! black, or pied, or brown;
Hither, ye furred ones! Hither every beast!
Only to one of all my forest clan
I cry, "Avaunt! Our mourning revels flee!"
On the grey wolf I lay my sovereign ban,
The great grey wolf with scraping claws, lest he
Lay bare my dead, for gloating foes to see—
Lay bare my dead, who died, and died for me.

Hon. Emily Lawless

O'Hussey's Ode to the Maguire

Where is my Chief, my master, this bleak night,
   mavrone!
O, cold, cold, miserably cold is this bleak night for
   Hugh,
Its showery, arrowy, speary sleet pierceth one
   through and through,
Pierceth one to the very bone!

Rolls real thunder? Or was that red, livid light
Only a meteor? I scarce know; but through the
   midnight dim
The pitiless ice-wind streams. Except the hate that
   persecutes *him*
Nothing hath crueller venomy might.

An awful, a tremendous night is this, meseems!
The flood-gates of the rivers of heaven, I think,
   have been burst wide—
Down from the overcharged clouds, like unto
   headlong ocean's tide,
Descends grey rain in roaring streams.

Though he were even a wolf ranging the round
  green woods,
Though he were even a pleasant salmon in the
  unchainable sea,
Though he were a wild mountain eagle, he could
  scarce bear, he,
This sharp, sore sleet, these howling floods.

O, mournful is my soul this night for Hugh
  Maguire!
Darkly, as in a dream, he strays! Before him and
  behind
Triumphs the tyrannous anger of the wounding
  wind,
The wounding wind, that burns as fire!

It is my bitter grief—it cuts me to the heart—
That in the country of Clan Darry this should be
  his fate!
O, woe is me, where is he? Wandering, houseless,
  desolate,
Alone, without or guide or chart!

Medreams I see just now his face, the
  strawberry-bright,
Uplifted to the blackened heavens, while the
  tempestuous winds

Blow fiercely over and around him, and the
    smiting sleet-shower blinds
The hero of Galang to-night!

Large, large affliction unto me and mine it is,
That one of his majestic bearing, his fair, stately
    form,
Should thus be tortured and o'erborne—that this
    unsparing storm
Should wreak its wrath on head like his!

That his great hand, so oft the avenger of the
    oppressed,
Should this chill, churlish night, perchance, be
    paralysed by frost—
While through some icicle-hung thicket—as one
    lorn and lost—
He walks and wanders without rest.

The tempest-driven torrent deluges the mead,
It overflows the low banks of the rivulets and ponds—
The lawns and pasture-grounds lie locked in icy
    bonds
So that the cattle cannot feed.

The pale bright margins of the streams are seen
    by none.

Rushes and sweeps along the untamable flood on
    every side—
It penetrates and fills the cottagers' dwellings far
    and wide—
Water and land are blent in one.

Through some dark woods, 'mid bones of
    monsters, Hugh now strays,
As he confronts the storm with anguished heart,
    but manly brow—
O! what a sword-wound to that tender heart of his
    were now
A backward glance at peaceful days.

But other thoughts are his—thoughts that can still
    inspire
With joy and an onward-bounding hope the
    bosom of Mac-Nee—
Thoughts of his warriors charging like bright
    billows of the sea,
Borne on the wind's wings, flashing fire!

And though frost glaze to-night the clear dew of
    his eyes,
And white ice-gauntlets glove his noble fine fair
    fingers o'er,

A warm dress is to him that lightning-garb he ever
    wore,
The lightning of the soul, not skies.

AVRAN

Hugh marched forth to the fight—I grieved to see
    him so depart;
And lo! to-night he wanders frozen, rain-drenched,
    sad, betrayed—
*But the memory of the lime-white mansions his right
    hand hath laid*
In ashes warms the hero's heart!

James Clarence Mangan,
(From the Irish of O'Hussey)

CIII

Lament for the Death of
Eoghan Ruadh O'Neill

"Did they dare, did they dare, to slay Owen Roe
    O'Neill?"
"Yes, they slew with poison him they feared to
    meet with steel."
"May God wither up their hearts! May their blood
    cease to flow!

157

May they walk in living death, who poisoned
Owen Roe!

"Though it break my heart to hear, say again the
bitter words."
"From Derry, against Cromwell, he marched to
measure swords;
But the weapon of the Saxon met him on his way,
And he died at Cloc Uactair, upon Saint
Leonard's Day."

"Wail, wail ye for the Mighty One! Wail, wail ye
for the Dead!
Quench the hearth, and hold the breath—with
ashes strew the head!
How tenderly we loved him! How deeply we
deplore!
Holy Saviour! but to think we shall never see him
more!

"Sagest in the council was he, kindest in the hall:
Sure we never won a battle—'twas Owen won
them all.
Had he lived, had he lived, our dear country had
been free;
But he's dead, but he's dead, and 'tis slaves we'll
ever be.

"O'Farell and Clanrickard, Preston and Red Hugh,
Audley and MacMahon, ye are valiant, wise, and
    true;
But what—what are ye all to our darling who is
    gone?
The rudder of our ship was he—our castle's
    corner-stone!

"Wail, wail him through the island! Weep, weep for
    our pride!
Would that on the battle-field our gallant chief
    had died!
Weep the victor of Beinn Burb—weep him, young
    men and old!
Weep for him, ye women—your Beautiful lies cold!

"We thought you would not die—we were sure
    you would not go,
And leave us in our utmost need to Cromwell's
    cruel blow—
Sheep without a shepherd, when the snow shuts
    out the sky—
Oh, why did you leave us, Owen? why did you die?

"Soft as woman's was your voice, O'Neill! bright
    was your eye!
Oh! why did you leave us, Owen? why did you die?

Your troubles are all over—you're at rest with God
    on high;
But we're slaves, and we're orphans, Owen!—why
    did you die?"

Thomas Osborne Davis

Lament of O'Sullivan Bear

The sun on Ivera
    No longer shines brightly;
The voice of her music
    No longer is sprightly;
No more to her maidens
    The light dance is dear,
Since the death of our darling
    O'Sullivan Bear.

Scully! thou false one,
    You basely betrayed him,
In his strong hour of need,
    When thy right hand should aid him;
He fed thee—he clad thee—

You had all could delight thee:
You left him—you sold him—
    May heaven requite thee!

Scully! may all kinds
    Of evil attend thee!
On thy dark road of life
    May no kind one befriend thee!
May fevers long burn thee,
    And agues long freeze thee!
May the strong hand of God
    In his red anger seize thee!

Had he died calmly,
    I would not deplore him;
Or if the wild strife
    Of the sea-war closed o'er him;
But with ropes round his white limbs
    Through ocean to trail him,
Like a fish after slaughter—
    'Tis therefore I wail him.

Long may the curse
    Of his people pursue them;
Scully, that sold him,
    And soldier that slew him!
One glimpse of heaven's light

May they see never!
May the hearthstone of hell
  Be their best bed for ever!

In the hole which the vile hands
  Of soldiers had made thee,
Unhonoured, unshrouded,
  And headless they laid thee;
No sigh to regret thee,
  No eye to rain o'er thee,
No dirge to lament thee!
  No friend to deplore thee!

Dear head of my darling,
  How gory and pale,
These aged eyes see thee,
  High spiked on their gaol!
That cheek in the summer sun
  Ne'er shall grow warm;
Nor that eye e'er catch light,
  But the flash of the storm.

A curse, blessed ocean,
  Is on thy green water,
From the haven of Cork,
  To Ivera of slaughter:
Since thy billows were dyed

With the red wounds of fear
Of Muiertach Oge
Our O'Sullivan Bear.

Jeremiah Joseph Callanan
(From the Irish)

Clare Coast

Circa 1720

See, cold island, we stand
Here to-night on your shore,
To-night, but never again;
Lingering a moment more.
See, beneath us our boat
Tugs at its tightening chain,
Holds out its sail to the breeze,
Pants to be gone again.
Off then with shouts and mirth,
Off with laughter and jests,
Mirth and song on our lips,
Hearts like lead in our breasts.

Death and the grave behind,
Death and a traitor's bier;

Honour and fame before,
Why do we linger here?
Why do we stand and gaze,
Fools, whom fools despise,
Fools untaught by the years,
Fools renounced by the wise?
Heartsick, a moment more,
Heartsick, sorry, fierce,
Lingering, lingering on,
Dreaming the dreams of yore;
Dreaming the dreams of our youth,
Dreaming the days when we stood
Joyous, expectant, serene,
Glad, exultant of mood,
Singing with hearts afire,
Singing with joyous strain,
Singing aloud in our pride,
"We shall redeem her again!"
Ah, not to-night that strain,—
Silent to-night we stand,
A scanty, a toil-worn crew,
Strangers, foes in the land!
Gone the light of our youth,
Gone for ever, and gone
Hope with the beautiful eyes,
Who laughed as she lured us on;

Lured us to danger and death,
To honour, perchance to fame,—
Empty fame at the best,
Glory half dimmed with shame.
War-battered dogs are we
Fighters in every clime,
Fillers of trench and of grave,
Mockers, bemocked by time.
War-dogs, hungry and grey,
Gnawing a naked bone,
Fighters in every clime,
Every cause but our own.

See us, cold isle of our love!
Coldest, saddest of isles—
Cold as the hopes of our youth,
Cold as your own wan smiles.
Coldly your streams outpour,
Each apart on the height,
Trickling, indifferent, slow,
Lost in the hush of the night.
Colder, sadder the clouds,
Comfortless bringers of rain;
Desolate daughters of air,
Sweep o'er your sad grey plain
Hiding the form of your hills,

Hiding your low sand duns;
But coldest, saddest, oh isle!
Are the homeless hearts of your sons.

Coldest, and saddest there,
In yon sun-lit land of the south,
Where we sicken, and sorrow, and pine,
And the jest flies from mouth to mouth,
And the church bells crash overhead,
And the idle hours flit by,
And the beaded wine-cups clink,
And the sun burns fierce in the sky;
And your exiles, the merry of heart,
Laugh and boast with the best,—
Boast, and extol their part,
Boast, till some lifted brow,
Crossed with a line severe,
Seems with displeasure to ask,
"Are these loud braggarts we hear,
Are they the sons of the West,
The wept-for, the theme of songs,
The exiled, the injured, the banned,
The men of a thousand wrongs?"

Fool, did you never hear
Of sunshine which broke through rain?
Sunshine which came with storm?
Laughter that rang of pain?
Boastings begotten of grief,
Vauntings to hide a smart,
Braggings with trembling lip,
Tricks of a broken heart?

Sudden some wayward gleam,
Sudden some passing sound,—
The careless splash of an oar,
The idle bark of a hound,
A shadow crossing the sun,
An unknown step in the hall,
A nothing, a folly, a straw!—
Back it returns—all—all!
Back with the rush of a storm,
Back the old anguish and ill,
The sad, green landscape of home,
The small grey house by the hill,
The wide grey shores of the lake,
The low sky, seeming to weave
Its tender pitiful arms
Round the sick lone landscape at eve.
Back with its pains and its wrongs,

Back with its toils and its strife,
Back with its struggles and woe,
Back flows the stream of our life.
Darkened with treason and wrong,
Darkened with anguish and ruth,
Bitter, tumultuous, fierce,
Yet glad in the light of our youth.

So, cold island, we stand
Here to-night on your shore,—
To-night, but never again,
Lingering a moment more.
See, beneath us our boat
Tugs at its tightening chain,
Holds out its sail to the breeze,
Pants to be gone again.
Off then with shouts and mirth,
Off with laughter and jests,
Jests and song on our lips,
Hearts like lead in our breasts.

Hon. Emily Lawless

Wake of William Orr

Here our murdered brother lies—
Wake him not with women's cries;
Mourn the way that manhood ought;
Sit in silent trance of thought.

Write his merits on your mind—
Morals pure and manners kind;
In his head, as on a hill,
Virtue placed her citadel.

Why cut off in palmy youth?
Truth he spoke, and acted truth—
"Countrymen, Unite!" he cried,
And died—for what his Saviour died.

Who is she with aspect wild?
The widowed mother with her child—
Child new stirring in the womb!
Husband waiting for the tomb!

Angel of this sacred place,
Calm her soul and whisper peace,
Cord or axe or guillotin'
Make the sentence—not the sin.

Here we watch our brother's sleep;
Watch with us but do not weep;
Watch with us through dead of night,
But expect the morning light.

Conquer fortune—persevere!—
Lo! it breaks, the morning clear!
The cheerful cock awakes the skies,
The day is come—arise!—arise!

William Drennan

CVII

The Convict of Clonmel

How hard is my fortune,
    And vain my repining!
The strong rope of fate
    For this young neck is twining.
My strength is departed;
    My cheek sunk and sallow;
While I languish in chains,
    In the gaol of Clonmala.

No boy in the village
    Was ever yet milder,
I'd play with a child,

And my sport would be wilder.
I'd dance without tiring
  From morning till even,
And the goal-ball I'd strike
  To the lightning of Heaven.

At my bed-foot decaying,
  My hurl-bat is lying,
Through the boys of the village
  My goal-ball is flying;
My horse 'mong the neighbours
  Neglected may fallow,—
While I pine in my chains,
  In the gaol of Clonmala.

Next Sunday the patron
  At home will be keeping,
And the young active hurlers
  The field will be sweeping.
With the dance of fair maidens
  The evening they'll hallow,
While this heart, once so gay,
  Shall be cold in Clonmala.

Jeremiah Joseph Callanan
(From the Irish)

The Croppy Boy

It was early, early in the spring,
The birds did whistle and sweetly sing,
Changing their notes from tree to tree,
And the song they sang was Old Ireland free.

It was early, early in the night,
The yeoman cavalry gave me a fright;
The yeoman cavalry was my downfall
And taken was I by Lord Cornwall.

'Twas in the guard-house where I was laid
And in a parlour where I was tried;
My sentence passed and my courage low
When to Dungannon I was forced to go.

As I was passing my father's door,
My brother William stood at the door;
My aged father stood at the door,
And my tender mother her hair she tore.

As I was walking up Wexford Street
My own first cousin I chanced to meet;
My own first cousin did me betray,
And for one bare guinea swore my life away.

My sister Mary heard the express,
She ran upstairs in her morning-dress—
Five hundred guineas I will lay me down,
To see my brother safe in Wexford Town.

As I was walking up Wexford Hill,
Who could blame me to cry my fill?
I looked behind and I looked before,
But my tender mother I shall ne'er see more.

As I was mounted on the platform high,
My aged father was standing by;
My aged father did me deny,
And the name he gave me was the Croppy Boy.

It was in Dungannon this young man died,
And in Dungannon his body lies;
And you good Christians that do pass by
Just drop a tear for the Croppy Boy.

Anonymous

The Rising of the Moon

"O, then tell me, Shawn O'Farrall,
    Tell me why you hurry so?"
"Hush, ma bouchal, hush and listen;"
    And his cheeks were all a-glow:
"I bear orders from the Captain—
    Get you ready quick and soon;
For the pikes must be together
    At the Rising of the Moon."

"O, then tell me, Shawn O'Farrall,
    Where the gathering is to be?"
"In the oul' spot by the river
    Right well known to you and me;
One word more—for signal token
    Whistle up the marching tune,
With your pike upon your shoulder.
    At the Rising of the Moon."

Out from many a mud-wall cabin
    Eyes were watching through the night:
Many a manly chest was throbbing
    For the blessed warning light;

Murmurs passed along the valley
  Like the Banshee's lonely croon,
And a thousand blades were flashing
  At the Rising of the Moon.

There, beside the singing river,
  That dark mass of men were seen—
Far above the shining weapons
  Hung their own beloved green.
Death to every foe and traitor!
  Forward! strike the marching tune,
And hurrah, my boys, for freedom!
  'Tis the Rising of the Moon.

Well they fought for poor Old Ireland,
  And full bitter was their fate;
(Oh! what glorious pride and sorrow
  Fill the name of Ninety-Eight!)
Yet, thank God, e'en still are beating
  Hearts in manhood's burning noon,
Who would follow in their footsteps
  At the Rising of the Moon.

                              John Keegan Casey

By Memory Inspired

By memory inspired,
And love of country fired,
The deeds of men I love to dwell upon;
And the patriotic glow
Of my spirit must bestow
A tribute to O'Connell that is gone, boys—gone:
Here's a memory to the friends that are gone!

In October Ninety-seven—
May his soul find rest in Heaven!—
William Orr to execution was led on:
The jury, drunk, agreed
That Irish was his creed;
For perjury and threats drove them on, boys—on:
Here's the memory of John Mitchell that is gone!

In Ninety-eight—the month July—
The informer's pay was high;
When Reynolds gave the gallows brave MacCann;
But MacCann was Reynolds' first—
One could not allay his thirst;
So he brought up Bond and Byrne, that are gone,
    boys—gone:
Here's the memory of the friends that are gone!

We saw a nation's tears
        Shed for John and Henry Shears;
Betrayed by Judas, Captain Armstrong;
        We may forgive, but yet
        We never can forget
The poisoning of Maguire that is gone, boys—gone:
Our high Star and true Apostle that is gone!

        How did Lord Edward die?
        Like a man, without a sigh;
But he left his handiwork on Major Swan!
        But Sirr, with steel-clad breast,
        And coward heart at best,
Left us cause to mourn Lord Edward that is gone,
        boys—gone:
Here's the memory of our friends that are gone!

        September Eighteen-three,
        Closed this cruel history,
When Emmet's blood the scaffold flowed upon:
        Oh, had their spirits been wise,
        They might then realise
Their freedom! But we drink to Mitchell that is
        gone, boys—gone:
Here's the memory of the friends that are gone!

Anonymous

The Memory of the Dead⋆

Who fears to speak of Ninety-eight?
Who blushes at the name?
When cowards mock the patriot's fate,
Who hangs his head for shame?
He's all a knave, or half a slave,
Who slights his country thus;
But a true man, like you, man,
Will fill your glass with us.

We drink the memory of the brave,
The faithful and the few;
Some lie far off beyond the wave,
Some sleep in Ireland, too;
All, all are gone; but still lives on
The fame of those who died;
All true men, like you, men,
Remember them with pride.

Some on the shores of distant lands
Their weary hearts have laid,
And by the stranger's heedless hands
Their lonely graves were made;

⋆ See note, p. 397

But, though their clay be far away
Beyond the Atlantic foam,
In true men, like you, men,
Their spirit's still at home.

The dust of some is Irish earth,
Among their own they rest,
And the same land that gave them birth
Has caught them to her breast;
And we will pray that from their clay
Full many a race may start
Of true men, like you, men,
To act as brave a part.

They rose in dark and evil days
To right their native land;
They kindled here a living blaze
That nothing shall withstand.
Alas! that might can vanquish right—
They fell and passed away;
But true men, like you, men,
Are plenty here to-day.

Then here's their memory! may it be
For us a guiding light,
To cheer our strife for liberty,
And teach us to unite—

Through good and ill, be Ireland's still,
    Though sad as theirs your fate,
And true men be you, men,
    Like those of Ninety-eight.

John Kells Ingram

Lament for Thomas Davis

I walked through Ballinderry in the spring-time,
    When the bud was on the tree;
And I said, in every fresh-ploughed field beholding
    The sowers striding free,
Scattering broadside forth the corn in golden
        plenty
On the quick seed-clasping soil
"Even such, this day, among the fresh-stirred
        hearts of Erin,
    Thomas Davis, is thy toil!"

I sat by Ballyshannon in the summer,
    And saw the salmon leap;
And I said, as I beheld the gallant creatures
    Spring glittering from the deep,

Through the spray, and through the prone heaps
    striving onward
  To the calm clear streams above,
"So seekest thou thy native founts of freedom,
    Thomas Davis,
  In thy brightness of strength and love!"

I stood on Derrybawn in the autumn,
  And I heard the eagle call,
With a clangorous cry of wrath and lamentation
  That filled the wide mountain hall,
O'er the bare deserted place of his plundered eyrie;
  And I said as he screamed and soared,
"So callest thou, thou wrathful soaring Thomas
    Davis,
  For a nation's rights restored!"

And alas! to think but now, and thou art lying,
  Dear Davis, dead at thy mother's knee;
And I, no mother near, on my own sick-bed,
  That face on earth shall never see;
I may lie and try to feel that I am dreaming,
  I may lie and try to say, "Thy will be done"—
But a hundred such as I will never comfort Erin
  For the loss of the noble son!

Young husbandman of Erin's fruitful seed-time,
  In the fresh track of danger's plough!
Who will walk the heavy, toilsome, perilous furrow
  Girt with freedom's seed-sheets now?
Who will banish with the wholesome crop of
    knowledge
  The daunting weed and the bitter thorn,
Now that thou thyself art but a seed for hopeful
    planting
  Against the Resurrection morn?

Young salmon of the flood-tide of freedom
  That swells round Erin's shore!
Thou wilt leap against their loud oppressive torrent
  Of bigotry and hate no more;
Drawn downward by their prone material instinct,
  Let them thunder on their rocks and foam—
Thou hast leapt, aspiring soul, to founts beyond
    their raging,
  Where troubled waters never come.

But I grieve not, Eagle of the empty eyrie,
  That thy wrathful cry is still;
And that the songs alone of peaceful mourners
  Are heard to-day on Erin's hill;
Better far, if brothers' war be destined for us,
  (God avert that horrid day, I pray),

That ere our hands be stained with slaughter
  fratricidal
  Thy warm heart should be cold in clay.

But my trust is strong in God, Who made us
  brothers,
  That He will not suffer their right hands
Which thou hast joined in holier rites than
  wedlock
  To draw opposing brands.
Oh, many a tuneful tongue that thou mad'st vocal
  Would lie cold and silent then;
And songless long once more, should often-
  widowed Erin
  Mourn the loss of her brave young men.

Oh, brave young men, my love, my pride, my
  promise,
  'Tis on you my hopes are set,
In manliness, in kindliness, in justice,
  To make Erin a nation yet,
Self-respecting, self-relying, self-advancing,
  In union or in severance, free and strong—
And if God grant this, then, under God, to
  Thomas Davis
  Let the greater praise belong.

Sir Samuel Ferguson

When I was a Little Girl

When I was a little girl,
In a garden playing,
A thing was often said
To chide us delaying:

When after sunny hours,
At twilight's falling,
Down through the garden walks
Came our old nurse calling.

"Come in! for it's growing late,
And the grass will wet ye!
Come in! or when it's dark
The Fenians will get ye."

Then, at this dreadful news,
All helter-skelter,
The panic-struck little flock
Ran home for shelter.

And round the nursery fire
Sat still to listen,
Fifty bare toes on the hearth,
Ten eyes a-glisten.

To hear of a night in March,
And loyal folk waiting,
To see a great army of men
Come devastating.

An army of Papists grim,
With a green flag o'er them,
Red-coats and black police
Flying before them.

But God (Who our nurse declared
Guards British dominions)
Sent down a deep fall of snow
And scattered the Fenians.

"But somewhere they're lurking yet,
Maybe they're near us,"
Four little hearts pit-a-pat
Thought "Can they hear us?"

Then the wind-shaken pane
Sounded like drumming;
"Oh!" they cried, "tuck us in,
The Fenians are coming!"

Four little pairs of hands
In the cots where she led those,
Over their frightened heads
Pulled up the bedclothes.

But one little rebel there,
Watching all with laughter,
Thought "When the Fenians come
I'll rise and go after."

Wished she had been a boy
And a good deal older—
Able to walk for miles
With a gun on her shoulder.

Able to lift aloft
The Green Flag o'er them
(Red-coats and black police
Flying before them).

And, as she dropped asleep,
Was wondering whether
God, if they prayed to Him,
Would give fine weather.

Alice Milligan

The Land War

Prelude

Sorrow is over the fields,
The fields that can never know
The joy that the harvest yields
When the corn stands row on row.

But alien the cattle feed
Where many a furrow lies,
For the furrows remember the seed,
And the men have a dream in their eyes.

Not so did the strong men dream
Ere the fathers of these were born,
And their sons have remembered their deeds
As the fields have remembered the corn.

Seumas O'Sullivan

Thomas MacDonagh

He shall not hear the bittern cry
In the wild sky, where he is lain,
Nor voices of the sweeter birds
Above the wailing of the rain.

Nor shall he know when loud March blows
Thro' slanting snows her fanfare shrill,
Blowing to flame the golden cup
Of many an upset daffodil.

But when the Dark Cow leaves the moor,
And pastures poor with greedy weeds,
Perhaps he'll hear her low at morn
Lifting her horn in pleasant meads.

Francis Ledwidge

Cairn Builders

For Easter 1916

What do they here then
  These, who arise
Out of the wild glen,
  Into the waste grey skies—
Be these most distraught men,
  Be they most wise?

With what unknown prayer
  Climbs each alone,
Into the chill air,
  Within his hands a stone—
What mysteries prepare,
  What rites intone?

Rear they an altar high,
  Build they a tomb?
They are passed, utterly;
  Within the wind's vast womb.
Only the curlew's cry,
  And bitter spume.

An Pilibin

Easter 1916

I have met them at close of day
Coming with vivid faces
From counter or desk among grey
Eighteenth-century houses.
I have passed with a nod of the head
Or polite meaningless words,
Or have lingered awhile and said
Polite meaningless words,
And thought before I had done
Of a mocking tale or a gibe
To please a companion
Around the fire at the club,
Being certain that they and I
But lived where motley is worn:
All changed, changed utterly:
A terrible beauty is born.

That woman's days were spent
In ignorant good will,
Her nights in argument
Until her voice grew shrill.
What voice more sweet than hers
When young and beautiful,

She rode to harriers?
This man had kept a school
And rode our winged horse;
This other his helper and friend
Was coming into his force;
He might have won fame in the end,
So sensitive his nature seemed,
So daring and sweet his thought.
This other man I had dreamed
A drunken, vainglorious lout.
He had done most bitter wrong
To some who are near my heart,
Yet I number him in the song;
He, too, has resigned his part
In the casual comedy;
He, too, has been changed in his turn,
Transformed utterly:
A terrible beauty is born.

Hearts with one purpose alone
Through summer and winter seem
Enchanted to a stone
To trouble the living stream.
The horse that comes from the road,
The rider, the birds that range
From cloud to tumbling cloud,

Minute by minute they change;
A shadow of cloud on the stream
Changes minute by minute;
A horse-hoof slides on the brim,
And a horse plashes within it
Where long-legged moorhens dive,
And hens to moorcocks call.
Minute by minute they live:
The stone's in the midst of all.

Too long a sacrifice
Can make a stone of the heart.
O when may it suffice?
That is heaven's part, our part
To murmur name upon name,
As a mother names her child
When sleep at last has come
On limbs that had run wild.
What is it but nightfall?
No, no, not night but death;
Was it needless death after all?
For England may keep faith
For all that is done and said.
We know their dream; enough
To know they dreamed and are dead;
And what if excess of love

Bewildered them till they died?
I write it out in a verse—
MacDonagh and MacBride
And Connolly and Pearse
Now and in time to be,
Wherever green is worn,
Are changed, changed utterly:
A terrible beauty is born.

W. B. Yeats

CXVIII
Cean Duv Deelish

Cean duv deelish, beside the sea
I stand and stretch my hands to thee
  Across the world.
The riderless horses race to shore
With thundering hoofs and shuddering, hoar,
  Blown manes uncurled.

Cean duv deelish, I cry to thee
Beyond the world, beneath the sea,
  Thou being dead.

Where hast thou hidden from the beat
Of crushing hoofs and tearing feet
    Thy dear black head?

Cean duv deelish, 'tis hard to pray
With breaking heart from day to day,
    And no reply;
When the passionate challenge of sky is cast
In the teeth of the sea and an angry blast
    Goes keening by.

God bless the woman, whoever she be,
From the tossing waves will recover thee
    And lashing wind.
Who will take thee out of the wind and storm,
Dry thy wet face on her bosom warm
    And lips so kind?

I not to know. It is hard to pray,
But I shall for this woman from day to day,
    "Comfort my dead,
The sport of the winds and the play of the sea."
I loved thee too well for this thing to be,
    O dear black head!

                Dora Sigerson Shorter

I am Ireland

I am Ireland,
Older than the Hag of Beara.

Great my pride,
I gave birth to brave Cuchulain.

Great my shame,
My own children killed their mother.

I am Ireland,
Lonelier than the Hag of Beara.

Lady Gregory
(From the Irish of Padraig Pearse)

CXX

Inis Fál

Now may we turn aside and dry our tears,
And comfort us, and lay aside our fears,
For all is gone—all comely quality,
All gentleness and hospitality,
All courtesy and merriment is gone;
Our virtues all are withered every one,

Our music vanished and our skill to sing:
Now may we quiet us and quit our moan,
Nothing is whole that could be broke; nothing
Remains to us of all that was our own.

James Stephens
(From the Irish of Egan O'Rahilly)

CXXI

A Lament for Ireland

I do not know of anything under the sky
That is friendly or favourable to the Gael,
But only the sea that our need brings us to,
Or the wind that blows to the harbour
The ship that is bearing us away from Ireland;
And there is reason that these are reconciled
    with us,
For we increase the sea with our tears,
And the wandering wind with our sighs.

Lady Gregory
(From the Irish of Shemus Cartan)

Dark Rosaleen

O my Dark Rosaleen,
    Do not sigh, do not weep!
The priests are on the ocean green,
    They march along the Deep.
There's wine . . . from the royal Pope
    Upon the ocean green;
And Spanish ale shall give you hope,
    My Dark Rosaleen!
    My own Rosaleen!
Shall glad your heart, shall give you hope,
Shall give you health, and help, and hope,
    My Dark Rosaleen.

Over hills and through dales
    Have I roamed for your sake;
All yesterday I sailed with sails
    On river and on lake.
The Erne . . . at its highest flood
    I dashed across unseen,
For there was lightning in my blood,
    My Dark Rosaleen!
    My own Rosaleen!

Oh! there was lightning in my blood,
Red lightning lightened through my blood,
    My Dark Rosaleen!

All day long in unrest
    To and fro do I move,
The very soul within my breast
    Is wasted for you, love!
The heart . . . in my bosom faints
    To think of you, my Queen,
My life of life, my saint of saints,
    My Dark Rosaleen!
    My own Rosaleen!
To hear your sweet and sad complaints,
My life, my love, my saint of saints,
    My Dark Rosaleen!

Woe and pain, pain and woe,
    Are my lot night and noon,
To see your bright face clouded so,
    Like to the mournful moon.
But yet . . . will I rear your throne
    Again in golden sheen;
'Tis you shall reign, shall reign alone,
    My Dark Rosaleen!
    My own Rosaleen!

'Tis you shall have the golden throne,
'Tis you shall reign, and reign alone,
　　My Dark Rosaleen!

Over dews, over sands
　　Will I fly for your weal;
Your holy delicate white hands
　　Shall girdle me with steel.
At home . . . in your emerald bowers,
　　From morning's dawn till e'en,
You'll pray for me, my flower of flowers,
　　My Dark Rosaleen!
　　My fond Rosaleen!
You'll think of me through Daylight's hours,
My virgin flower, my flower of flowers,
　　My Dark Rosaleen!

I could scale the blue air,
　　I could plough the high hills,
Oh, I could kneel all night in prayer,
　　To heal your many ills!
And one . . . beamy smile from you
　　Would float like light between
My toils and me, my own, my true,
　　My Dark Rosaleen!
　　My fond Rosaleen!

Would give me life and soul anew,
A second life, a soul anew,
    My Dark Rosaleen!

O! the Erne shall run red
    With redundance of blood,
The earth shall rock beneath our tread,
    And flames wrap hill and wood,
And gun-peal, and slogan cry,
    Wake many a glen serene,
Ere you shall fade, ere you shall die,
    My Dark Rosaleen!
    My own Rosaleen!
The Judgment Hour must first be nigh,
Ere you can fade, ere you can die,
    My Dark Rosaleen!

                    James Clarence Mangan
                    (From the Irish of Costello)

After Death

Shall mine eyes behold thy glory, oh, my country?
  Shall mine eyes behold thy glory?
Or shall the darkness close around them ere the
    sun-blaze
  Break at last upon thy story?

When the nations ope for thee their queenly circle,
  As sweet new sister hail thee,
Shall these lips be sealed in callous death and
    silence,
  That have known but to bewail thee?

Shall the ear be deaf that only loved thy praises,
  When all men their tribute bring thee?
Shall the mouth be clay that sang thee in thy
    squalor,
  When all poets' mouths shall sing thee?

Ah! the harpings and the salvos and the shoutings
  Of thy exiled sons returning,
I should hear, tho' dead and mouldered, and the
    grave-damps
  Should not chill my bosom's burning.

Ah! the tramp of feet victorious! I should hear
    them
  'Mid the shamrocks and the mosses,
And my heart should toss within the shroud and
    quiver
  As a captive dreamer tosses.

I should turn and rend the cere-cloths round me—
  Giant sinews I should borrow—
Crying "Oh, my brothers, I have also loved her
  In her loneliness and sorrow!

"Let me join with you the jubilant procession,
  Let me chant with you her story;
Then, contented, I shall go back to the shamrocks,
  Now mine eyes have seen her glory."

                                          Fanny Parnell

                      CXXIV

                 Cancel the Past

Cancel the past! Why, yes! We, too, have thought
Of conflict crowned and drowned in olives of peace;
But when Cuchullin and Ferdiadh fought
There lacked no pride of warrior courtesies,

                        202

And so must this fight end.
Bond, from the toil of hate we may not cease:
Free, we are free to be your friend.
And when you make your banquet, and we come,
Soldier with equal soldier must we sit,
Closing a battle, not forgetting it.
With not a name to hide,
This mate and mother of valiant "rebels" dead
Must come with all her history on her head.
We keep the past for pride:
No deepest peace shall strike our poets dumb:
No rawest squad of all Death's volunteers,
No rudest man who died
To tear your flag down in the bitter years,
But shall have praise, and three times thrice again,
When at that table men shall drink with men.

T. M. Kettle

CXXV
The Little Black Rose

The Little Black Rose shall be red at last;
  What made it black but the March wind dry,
And the tear of the widow that fell on it fast?
  It shall redden the hills when June is nigh.

The Silk of the Kine shall rest at last;
  What drove her forth but the dragon-fly?
In the golden vale she shall feed full fast,
  With her mild gold horn and her slow, dark eye.

The wounded wood-dove lies dead at last!
  The pine long bleeding, it shall not die!
This song is secret. Mine ear it passed
  In a wind o'er the plains at Athenry.

Aubrey de Vere

CXXVI

You Drop a Tear

You drop a tear for those that die.
To me, yet living, grant a sigh.
Surely they rest: no rest have I.

The sighing wind dies on the tree.
I cannot sigh: sigh thou for me.
The broken heart is sadly free.

You bid me say what I would have:
Will one flower serve? or do I crave
A wreath—to decorate a grave?

Fling poppies on the grave of Youth;
Fling pansies on the tomb of Truth;
On mine to-morrow morn fling both.

All day I sat below your gate,
My spirit calmed by its own weight;
Then Sorrow grew importunate.

I rose, and on the steps I writ
These fragments of a wildered wit:
To be erased beneath your feet.

Erase them, haughty feet—I live!
I wished, not hoped, that you might grieve.
You can forget: ah then, forgive!

Aubrey de Vere

Cold, Sharp Lamentation

Cold, sharp lamentation
In the cold bitter winds
Ever blowing across the sky;
Oh, there was loneliness with me!

The loud sounding of the waves
Beating against the shore,
Their vast, rough, heavy outcry,
Oh, there was loneliness with me!

The light sea-gulls in the air,
Crying sharply through the harbours,
The cries and screams of the birds
With my own heart! Oh! that was loneliness.

The voice of the winds and the tide,
And the long battle of the mighty war;
The sea, the earth, the skies, the blowing of the
    winds,
Oh! there was loneliness in all of them together.

Lady Gregory
(From the Irish of Douglas Hyde)

CXXVIII

The Sally Ring

Within the ring o' sallies
    The stream is dark an' slow;
'Tis deep an' dark with ne'er a croon
At night below the summer moon
    To tell it's life—an' so

Within the ring o' sallies
    The fairy fingers blow.

Within the ring o' sallies
    I heard the Whispers call—
'Tis lonesome there a summer day,
'Tis strange an' lonesome there alway
    Beside the broken wall
Within the ring o' sallies
    Where Whispers ever fall.

Within the ring o' sallies
    The years come home to die—
A thousand, thousand graves there be
That on'y fairies know an' see
    (Or maybe you an' I)
Within the ring o' sallies—
    An' there meself would lie.

Within the ring o' sallies
    I'll build a house o' stone,
A little house an' white with lime.
An' thatched with sedge o' yestertime,
    An' live me all alone
Within the ring o' sallies
    Where I was sometime known.

Patrick Kelly

To Morfydd

A voice on the winds,
A voice by the waters,
  Wanders and cries:
Oh! what are the winds?
And what are the waters?
  Mine are your eyes!

Western the winds are,
And western the waters,
  Where the light lies:
Oh! what are the winds?
And what are the waters?
  Mine are your eyes!

Cold, cold grow the winds,
And wild grow the waters,
  Where the sun dies:
Oh! what are the winds?
And what are the waters?
  Mine are your eyes!

And down the night winds,
And down the night waters,
  The music flies:

Oh! what are the winds?
And what are the waters?
Cold be the winds,
And wild be the waters,
So mine be your eyes!

Lionel Johnson

To a Child Dancing in the Wind

Dance there upon the shore;
What need have you to care
For wind or water's roar?
And tumble out your hair
That the salt drops have wet;
Being young you have not known
The fool's triumph, nor yet
Love lost as soon as won,
Nor the best labourer dead
And all the sheaves to bind.
What need have you to dread
The monstrous crying of wind?

W. B. Yeats

Two Years Later

Has no one said those daring
Kind eyes should be more learn'd?
Or warned you how despairing
The moths are when they are burned,
I could have warned you, but you are young,
So we speak a different tongue.

O you will take whatever's offered
And dream that all the world's a friend,
Suffer as your mother suffered,
Be as broken in the end.
But I am old and you are young,
And I speak a barbarous tongue.

W. B. Yeats

On the Death of a Recluse

Love drooped when Beauty fled the bower
 And languid closed the day,
Wept every little flower
 And turned its head away.

The wind spoke with a fallen tongue,
    The green reed sighed amain,
And sable forests swung
    Rude melody again.

Wild caves rang deep and rocks grew cold,
    Whilst rivers wept by them,
All nature's death-bells tolled
    A requiem! a requiem!

'Mid roaring brooks and dark moss-vales,
    Where speechless Thought abides,
Still her sweet spirit dwells,
    That knew no world besides.

Her form the woodland still retains—
    Wound but a creeping flower,
Her very life-blood stains
    Thee, in a falling shower.

Touch but the stream, drink but the air,
    Her cheek, her breath is known;
Ravish that red rose there,
    And she is all thine own.

George Darley

Love was True to Me

Love was true to me,
    True and tender;
I who ought to be
    Love's defender,
Let the cold winds blow
    Till they chilled him;
Let the winds and snow
Shroud him—and I know
    That I killed him.

Years he cried to me
    To be kinder;
I was blind to see
    And grew blinder.
Years with soft hands raised
    Fondly reaching,
Wept and prayed and praised,
    Still beseeching.

When he died I woke,
    God! how lonely,
When the grey dawn broke
    On one only.

Now beside Love's grave
        I am kneeling;
All he sought and gave
        I am feeling.

John Boyle O'Reilly

The Children of Lir

Out upon the sand-dunes thrive the coarse long
        grasses,
    Herons standing knee-deep in the brackish pool,
Overhead the sunset fire and flame amasses,
    And the moon to eastward rises pale and cool:
Rose and green about her, silver-grey and pearly,
    Chequered with the black rooks flying home to
        bed;
For, to wake at daybreak, birds must couch them
        early,
    And the day's a long one since the dawn was red.

On the chilly lakelet, in that pleasant gloaming,
    See the sad swans sailing: they shall have no rest:
Never a voice to greet them save the bittern's
        booming

Where the ghostly sallows sway against the West.
"Sister," saith the grey swan, "Sister, I am weary,"
    Turning to the white swan wet, despairing eyes;
"Oh," she saith, "my young one, oh," she saith,
      "my dearie,"
    Casts her wings about him with a storm of cries.

Woe for Lir's sweet children whom their vile
    stepmother
    Glamoured with her witch-spells for a thousand
      years;
Died their father raving, on his throne another,
    Blind before the end came from the burning
      tears.
Long the swans have wandered over lake and
    river.
    Gone is all the glory of the race of Lir,
Gone and long forgotten like a dream of fever:
    But the swans remember the sweet days that
      were.

Dews are in the clear air, and the roselight paling,
    Over sands and sedges shines the evening star,
And the moon's disc lonely high in heaven is
    sailing,

Silvered all the spear-heads of the rushes are,—
Housed warm are all things as the night grows
    colder,
  Water-fowl and sky-fowl dreamless in the nest;
But the swans go drifting, drooping wing and
    shoulder
  Cleaving the still water where the fishes rest.

Katharine Tynan

CXXXV

This Weariness and Grief

This weariness and grief
  Are going greatly, greatly, round my heart,
And the full of my two shoes of it,
  And the tears dropping down with me.
It is what I think the Sunday long from me,
  Oh, thousand treasures till you pass the way.
And my darling twice over you are,
  Giving farewell to you, until I return again.

Oh, affection, and oh, darling,
  In the beginning of the summer would you
    move with me yourself

Out among the valleys,
  Where we might be at the going-under of the
    sun.
Cows, sheep, or calves
  I would not ask them for fortune with thee,
But my hand beneath your white form,
  And leave to converse until twelve would strike.

A hundred farewells to last night;
  It is my grief that it was not to-night that was
    first.
A sprightly *bohaleen*
  That would coax me awhile on his knee.
I would tell you a tale myself
  If it were possible you could keep a secret for me,
That my love is forsaking me,
  Oh! bright God, and oh, Mary, is it not the pity!

Douglas Hyde
(From the Irish)

The White Wave Following

Like the white wave following
Our ship through changing waters,
The memory of your love is
In life that alters:
The clouds pass overhead,
And like clouds the islands
Flock up—and hurrying on
Float by on the blue of the ocean;
The sun goes, and the moon,
Along many mountains

Amid changing stars,
Into heaven uprolling,
New lochs and lands
In each hour illumines:
And all waves of the sea,
Tide-swept and wind-swayed
From morning unto night,
Move ceaselessly by us.

But against all winds
And all swift tide-races,
To all lochs and lands

And sea-girt lonely places,
Sunlit and moonlit,
Heaving and hollowing
Through wind-gleam, and glass-calm,
Comes one white wave following.

And like that white wave,
In the sunlit Sound of Jura,
Like that wave, bright-crested
Amid grey seas by Sanda,
On black rocks breaking
Around distant Rona,
Or in foam track fading
O'er a sea of slumber,
As we came from Canna
To Skye of your kindred:
Like that white wave, following
The ship through changing waters,
The memory of your love is
In life that alters.

Alice Milligan

Song

I made another garden, yea,
  For my new love;
I left the dead rose where it lay,
  And set the new above.
Why did the summer not begin?
  Why did my heart not haste?
My old love came and walked therein,
  And laid the garden waste.

She entered with her weary smile,
  Just as of old;
She looked around a little while,
  And shivered at the cold.
Her passing touch was death to all,
  Her passing look a blight:
She made the white rose-petals fall,
  And turned the red rose white.

Her pale robe, clinging to the grass,
  Seemed like a snake
That bit the grass and ground, alas!
  And a sad trail did make.
She went up slowly to the gate;

219

And there, just as of yore,
　She turned back at the last to wait,
And say farewell once more.

Arthur O'Shaughnessy

CXXXVIII

Requiescat

Tread lightly, she is near
　Under the snow,
Speak gently, she can hear
　The daisies grow.

All her bright golden hair
　Tarnished with rust,
She that was young and fair
　Fallen to dust.

Lily-like, white as snow,
　She hardly knew
She was a woman, so
　Sweetly she grew.

Coffin-board, heavy stone,
　Lie on her breast,
I vex my heart alone,
　She is at rest.

Peace, Peace, she cannot hear
        Lyre or sonnet,
All my life's buried here,
        Heap earth upon it.

Oscar Wilde

A Moment

"Was that the wind?" she said,
And turned her head
To where, on a green bank, the primrose flowers
Seemed with new beauty suddenly endowed,
As though they gazed out of their mortal cloud
On things unseen, communing with strange
        powers.

Then upon that green place
Fell a new grace,
As when a sun-gleam visits drops of dew,
And every drop shines like a mystic gem,
Set in the front of morning's diadem,
With hues more tender than e'er a diamond knew.

And something seemed to pass—
As through the grass
The presence of the gentlest wind will go—
Delicately through her bosom and her hair,
Till, with delight, she found herself more fair,
And her heart sang, unutterably low.

John Todhunter

CXL

A Sad Song

Love once kiss'd me,
Unfolded his wings, and fled.
   Hath friendship miss'd me?
Is faith in all friendship dead?
   If a spell could summon
These phantoms that come and go,
   Of men and women,
Their very selves to show,
   I might find (alas me!)
My seeking both night and day.
   But I pass them, they pass me,
And each on a lonely way.

Soul, art thou friendless,
A loser, sorrowful, weak?
Life is not endless,
Death is not far to seek.
Thou sailest ever,
Each moment, if sad or kind,
Down the great river;
It opens, it closes behind;
Far back see-est
The mountain-tops' faint azure;
Below, as thou flee-est,
The ripple, the shadow's erasure.

Why dost thou, weeping,
Stretch forth thine arms in vain?
It breaks thy sleeping;
O drop into trance again.
In dreams thou may'st go where
Child's Island is flowery grass'd,
Deep-skied,—it is nowhere
Save in the Land of the Past.
Time is dying,
The World too; forget their moan;
The sad wind sighing
Let murmur, this alone.

William Allingham

Le Jardin

The lily's withered chalice falls
 Around its rod of dusty gold,
 And from the beech-trees on the wold
The last wood-pigeon coos and calls.

The gaudy leonine sunflower
 Hangs black and barren on its stalk,
 And down the windy garden walk
The dead leaves scatter,—hour by hour.

Pale privet-petals white as milk
 Are blown into a snowy mass:
 The roses lie upon the grass
Like little shreds of crimson silk.

Oscar Wilde

Sarrazine's Song

Hath any loved you well; down there,
 Summer or winter through?
Down there, have you found any fair
 Laid in the grave with you?

Is death's long kiss a richer kiss
  Than mine was wont to be—
Or have you gone to some far bliss
  And quite forgotten me?

What soft enamouring of sleep
  Hath you in some soft way?
What charmed death holdeth you with deep
  Strange lure by night and day?
—A little space below the grass,
  Out of the sun and shade;
But worlds away from me, alas,
  Down there where you are laid.

My bright hair's waved and wasted gold,
  What is it now to thee—
Whether the rose-red life I hold
  Or white death holdeth me?
Down there you love the grave's own green,
  And evermore you rave
Of some sweet seraph you have seen
  Or dreamt of in the grave.

There you shall lie as you have lain,
  Though in the world above,
Another live your life again,
  Loving again your love:

Is it not sweet beneath the palm?
    Is not the warm day rife
With some long mystic golden calm
    Better than love and life?

The broad quaint odorous leaves like hands
    Weaving the fair day through,
Weave sleep no burnished bird withstands,
    While death weaves sleep for you;
And many a strange rich breathing sound
    Ravishes morn and noon:
And in that place you must have found
    Death a delicious swoon.

Hold me no longer for a word
    I used to say or sing:
Ah, long ago you must have heard
    So many a sweeter thing:
For rich earth must have reached your heart
    And turned the faith to flowers;
And warm wind stolen, part by part,
    Your soul through faithless hours.

And many a soft seed must have won
    Soil of some yielding thought,
To bring a bloom up to the sun
    That else had ne'er been brought;

And, doubtless, many a passionate hue
   Hath made that place more fair,
Making some passionate part of you
   Faithless to me down there.

Arthur O'Shaughnessy

Drought

The sky is greyer than doves,
Hardly a zephyr moves,
Little voices complain;
The leaves rustle before the rain.

No thrush is singing now,
All is still in the heart o' the bough;
Only the trembling cry
Of young leaves murmuring thirstily.

Only the moan and stir
Of little hands in the boughs I hear,
Beckoning the rain to come
Out of the evening, out of the gloom.

The wind's wings are still;
Nothing stirs but the singing rill
And hearts that complain.
The leaves rustle before the rain.

Katharine Tynan

Song

Girls, when I am gone away,
　On this bosom strew
Only flowers meek and pale,
　And the yew.

Lay these hands down by my side,
　Let my face be bare;
Bind a kerchief round the face,
　Smooth my hair.

Let my bier be borne at dawn,
　Summer grows so sweet,
Deep into the forest green
　Where boughs meet.

Then pass away, and let me lie
　　One long, warm, sweet day
There alone with face upturn'd,
　　One sweet day.

While the morning light grows broad,
　　While noon sleepeth sound,
While the evening falls and faints,
　　While the world goes round.

Edward Dowden

O Dreamy, Gloomy, Friendly Trees

O dreamy, gloomy, friendly Trees,
　　I came along your narrow track
To bring my gifts unto your knees
　　And gifts did you give back;
For when I brought this heart that burns—
　　These thoughts that bitterly repine—
And laid them here among the ferns
　　And the hum of boughs divine,
Ye, vastest breathers of the air,
　　Shook down with slow and mighty poise

Your coolness on the human care,
    Your wonder on its toys,
Your greenness on the heart's despair,
    Your darkness on its noise.

Herbert Trench

Hesperus

(After Sappho)

Upon the sober sky thy robes are spread,
    They drape the twilight, veil on quiet veil,
Until the lingering daylight all has fled
    Before thee, modest goddess, shadow-pale:
The hushed and reverent sky
Her diadem of stars has lifted high.

The tender lamb, the bleating kid, the fawn,
    All that the sunburnt day has scattered wide,
Thou dost regather, holding till the dawn
    Each flower and tree and beast unto thy side:
The sheep come to the pen,
The dreams come to the men,
    And to the mother's breast
    The tired child doth come and take his rest.

Evening gathers everything
    Scattered by the morning,
Fold for sheep and nest for wing,
Evening gathers everything,
Child to mother, queen to king
    Running at thy warning;
Evening gathers everything
    Scattered by the morning.

James Stephens

CXLVII

Refuge

Twilight, a timid fawn, went glimmering by,
    And Night, the dark-blue hunter, followed fast,
Ceaseless pursuit and flight were in the sky,
    But the long chase had ceased for us at last.

We watched together while the driven fawn
    Hid in the golden thicket of the day.
We, from whose hearts pursuit and flight were
    gone,
    Knew on the hunter's breast her refuge lay.

A. E.

Autumn

Slowly, one by one,
Through the damp-smelling, misty air of autumn
    the delicate leaves drop down,
Covering the grass like a carpet—
A carpet woven in gold and silver:—
And the sun,
Shining through the bare black trees,
Turns to a glory of gold these dying woods.

Ah! if any poet
Could stay that brief splendid vision,
Gather these autumn glories into his song,
What joy were his!
Let the winds scatter
The broken scarlet web of autumn wide over the
    world!
Soft with sleep,
Let the delicate air sigh through the naked
    branches,
That still preserve their beauty,
Though a barer, a more austere beauty than the
    green beauty of summer.

Now the sap of life runs low:
All that we did in life's spring-time and summer
  seems far away.
Faint as a dream, and quiet, the sports of those
  days—the shouts and the laughter.
Sad enough they seem
Now that we know well how brief and how fragile
  they were.
Gone, gone, is their merriment.
Only an echo remains while the curtain of night is
  descending;
But how lovely that echo!—
Lovelier far than the shouts and the laughter, the
  songs and the childish play:—
Lovely as autumn.

Forrest Reid

The Wild Swans at Coole

The trees are in their autumn beauty,
The woodland paths are dry,
Under the October twilight the water
Mirrors a still sky;

Upon the brimming water among the stones
Are nine and fifty swans.

The nineteenth Autumn has come upon me
Since I first made my count;
I saw, before I had well finished,
All suddenly mount
And scatter wheeling in great broken rings
Upon their clamorous wings.

I have looked upon those brilliant creatures,
And now my heart is sore.
All's changed since I, hearing at twilight,
The first time on this shore,
The bell-beat of their wings above my head,
Trod with a lighter tread

Unwearied still, lover by lover,
They paddle in the cold,
Companionable streams or climb the air;
Their hearts have not grown old;
Passion or conquest, wander where they will,
Attend upon them still.

But now they drift on the still water
Mysterious, beautiful;
Among what rushes will they build,

By what lake's edge or pool
Delight men's eyes when I awake some day
To find they have flown away?

W. B. Yeats

CL

The Church of a Dream

Sadly the dead leaves rustle in the whistling wind,
Around the weather-worn, grey church, low down
    the vale:
The Saints in golden vesture shake before the gale;
The glorious windows shake, where still they dwell
    enshrined;
Old Saints by long-dead, shrivelled hands, long
    since designed:
There still, although the world autumnal be, and
    pale,
Still in their golden vesture the old Saints prevail;
Alone with Christ, desolate else, left by mankind.

Only one ancient Priest offers the Sacrifice,
Murmuring holy Latin immemorial:
Swaying with tremulous hands the old censer full
    of spice,

In grey, sweet incense clouds; blue, sweet clouds
    mystical:
To him, in place of men, for he is old, suffice
Melancholy remembrances and vesperal.

Lionel Johnson

Remembrance

Cold in the earth—and the deep snow piled above
    thee,
Far, far, removed, cold in the dreary grave!
Have I forgot, my only Love, to love thee,
Severed at last by Time's all-severing wave?

Now, when alone, do my thoughts no longer hover
Over the mountains, on that northern shore,
Resting their wings where heath and fern-leaves
    cover
Thy noble heart for ever, ever more?

Cold in the earth—and fifteen wild Decembers,
From those brown hills, have melted into spring:
Faithful, indeed, is the spirit that remembers
After such years of change and suffering!

Sweet Love of youth, forgive, if I forget thee,
While the world's tide is bearing me along;
Other desires and other hopes beset me,
Hopes which obscure, but cannot do thee wrong!

No later light has lightened up my heaven,
No second morn has ever shone for me;
All my life's bliss from thy dear life was given,
All my life's bliss is in the grave with thee.

But, when the days of golden dreams had
        perished,
And even Despair was powerless to destroy;
Then did I learn how existence could be
        cherished,
Strengthened, and fed without the aid of joy.

Then did I check the tears of useless passion—
Weaned my young soul from yearning after thine;
Sternly denied its burning wish to hasten
Down to that tomb already more than mine.

And, even yet, I dare not let it languish,
Dare not indulge in memory's rapturous pain;
Once drinking deep of that divinest anguish,
How could I seek the empty world again?

                                    Emily Brontë

Love After Death

There is an earthly glimmer in the Tomb:
>   And, healed in their own tears and with long
>   sleep,
>   My eyes unclose and feel no need to weep;
But, in the corner of the narrow room,
Behold Love's spirit standeth, with the bloom
>   That things made deathless by Death's self
>   may keep.

>   O what a change! for now his looks are deep,
And a long patient smile he can assume:
While Memory, in some soft low monotone,
>   Is pouring like an oil into mine ear
>   The tale of a most short and hollow bliss,
That I once throbbed indeed to call my own,
>   Holding it hardly between joy and fear,—
>   And how that broke, and how it came to this.

Arthur O'Shaughnessy

Parting

As from our dream we died away
Far off I felt the outer things;
Your wind-blown tresses round me play,
Your bosom's gentle murmurings.

And far away our faces met
As on the verge of the vast spheres;
And in the night our cheeks were wet,
I could not say with dew or tears.

O gate by which I entered in!
O face and hair! O lips and eyes!
Through you again the world I win,
How far away from Paradise.

A. E.

The Sheep

Slowly they pass
In the grey of the evening
Over the wet road,
A flock of sheep.
Slowly they wend
In the grey of the gloaming,
Over the wet road
That winds through the town.
Slowly they pass,
And gleaming whitely
Vanish away
In the grey of the evening.
Ah, what memories
Loom for a moment,
Gleam for a moment,
And vanish away,
Of the white days
When we two together
Went in the evening,
Where the sheep lay:
We two together,
Went with slow feet

In the grey of the evening
Where the sheep lay.
Whitely they gleam
For a moment and vanish
Away in the dimness
Of sorrowful years:
Gleam for a moment,
All white, and go fading
Away in the greyness
Of sundering years.

Seumas O'Sullivan

The Fairy Fiddler

'Tis I go fiddling, fiddling,
  By weedy ways forlorn:
I make the blackbird's music
  Ere in his breast 'tis born:
The sleeping larks I waken
  Twixt the midnight and the morn.

No man alive has seen me,
  But women hear me play
Sometimes at door or window,

Fiddling the souls away,—
The child's soul and the colleen's
Out of the covering clay.

None of my fairy kinsmen
Make music with me now:
Alone the raths I wander
Or ride the whitethorn bough
But the wild swans they know me,
And the horse that draws the plough.

Nora Hopper

CLVI

Twilight

Far on the moor some wild bird screams—
The strange wild cry of homeless things—
A tired crane sails on listless wings
To her lone rest by silent streams.

Margaret Ryan

A Cradle Song

O, men from the fields!
Come gently within.
Tread softly, softly,
O! men coming in.

Mavourneen is going
From me and from you,
Where Mary will fold him
With mantle of blue!

From reek of the smoke
And cold of the floor,
And the peering of things
Across the half-door.

O, men from the fields!
Soft, softly come thro'.
Mary puts round him
Her mantle of blue.

Padraic Colum

No Child

I heard in the night the pigeons
    Stirring within their nest:
The wild pigeon's stir was tender,
    Like a child's hand at the breast.

I cried, "O, stir no more!
    (My breast was touched of tears),
O pigeons, make no stir—
    A childless woman hears."

Padraic Colum

CLIX

God's Remembrance

There came a whisper from the night to me
Like music of the sea, a mighty breath
From out of the valley's dewy mouth, and Death
Shook his lean bones, and every coloured tree
Wept in the fog of morning. From the town
Of nests among the branches one old crow
With gaps upon his wings flew far away,

And, thinking of the golden summer glow,
I heard a blackbird whistle half his lay
Among the spinning leaves that slanted down.

And I who am a thought of God's now long
Forgotten in His Mind, and desolate
With other dreams long over, as a gate
Singing upon the wind the anvil song,
Sang of the Spring when first He dreamt of me
In that old town all hills and signs that creak:—
And He remembered me as something far
In old imaginations, something weak
With distance, like a little sparkling star
Drowned in the lavender of evening sea.

Francis Ledwidge

CLX

At the Mid Hour of Night

At the mid hour of night, when stars are weeping,
    I fly
To the lone vale we loved, when life shone warm
    in thine eye;
And I think oft, if spirits can steal from the
    regions of air

To revisit past scenes of delight, thou wilt come to
    me there
And tell me our love is remembered, even in the
    sky!

Then I sing the wild song 'twas once such
    pleasure to hear!
When our voices, commingling, breathed like one
    on the ear;
And as Echo far off through the vale my sad
    orison rolls,
I think, Oh my love! 'tis thy voice from the
    Kingdom of Souls
Faintly answering still the notes that once were so
    dear.

Thomas Moore

CLXI

The Moon Worshippers

We are the partly real ones
Whose bodies are an accident,
Whose half-born souls were never meant
To fix their unsubstantial thrones
Inside a house of blood and bones.

All day we creep about the brain,
Benumbed and deafened with the noise
Of carnal pains and carnal joys,
That thrust their stupid joy and pain
Across the peace of our disdain.

But when the grosser senses swoon,
Then with dances privily,
And the wordless litany,
A million ghosts will importune
Our vestal mistress, lady Moon:

"O undefiled, O lucid Moon,
Hear our attenuated cry!
O little fish of the cold sky,
O swimmer of the void lagoon,
O Moon, shall our release be soon?"

E. R. Dodds

CLXII

The Secret Rose

Far off, most secret, and inviolate Rose,
Enfold me in my hour of hours; where those
Who sought thee in the Holy Sepulchre,
Or in the wine vat, dwell beyond the stir

And tumult of defeated dreams; and deep
Among pale eyelids, heavy with the sleep
Men have named beauty. Thy great leaves enfold
The ancient beards, the helms of ruby and gold
Of the crowned Magi; and the king whose eyes
Saw the Pierced Hands and Rood of elder rise
In Druid vapour and make the torches dim;
Till vain frenzy awoke and he died; and him
Who met Fand walking among flaming dew
By a grey shore where the wind never blew,
And lost the world and Emer for a kiss;
And him who drove the gods out of their liss,
And till a hundred morns had flowered red,
Feasted and wept the barrows of his dead;
And the proud dreaming king who flung the crown
And sorrow away, and calling bard and clown
Dwelt among wine-stained wanderers in deep
     woods;
And him who sold tillage, and house, and goods,
And sought through lands and islands numberless
     years,
Until he found with laughter and with tears,
A woman, of so shining loveliness,
That men threshed corn at midnight by a tress,
A little stolen tress. I, too, await

The hour of thy great wind of love and hate.
When shall the stars be blown about the sky,
Like the sparks blown out of a smithy, and die?
Surely thine hour has come, thy great wind blows.
Far off, most secret, and inviolate Rose?

W. B. Yeats

To the Moon

Oft have I thought and troubled not my head
   My eyelids heavy with thy mystery,
Death would but blow me from the feathery dead
   One heart-throb nearer thee.

Stoop down one night and try to break my heart!
   For all that you can say it may be whole.
Hush! Hush! Thou couldst not do it, for thou art
   Too close—my very soul.

H. Stuart

Complaint to the Moon

O lady of all the poems in the world!
Cast off thy graceful, effortless decay,
Who sing'st thy swan-song and with wing unfurled
Beat'st thy bright heart away;
O wound thyself and be for ever rid of
The drug, the opium that dulls thy veins,
That love may rise up stark about thee, love,
And grasp thy chariot reins.

H. Stuart

Night

Mysterious Night! When our first parent knew
Thee, from report divine, and heard thy name,
Did he not tremble for this lovely Frame,
This glorious canopy of Light and Blue?
Yet, 'neath a curtain of translucent dew,
Bathed in the rays of the great setting Flame,
Hesperus, with the Host of Heaven, came,
And lo! Creation widened on Man's view.

Who could have thought such darkness lay
    concealed
Within thy beams, O Sun! or who could find,
Whilst flower and leaf and insect stood revealed,
That to such countless orbs thou mad'st us blind!
Why do we then shun Death with anxious strife?
If Light can thus deceive, wherefore not Life?

Joseph Blanco White

CLXVI

Ardan Mór

As I was climbing Ardan Mór
From the shore of Sheelin lake,
I met the herons coming down
Before the waters wake.

And they were talking in their flight
Of dreamy ways the herons go
When all the hills are withered up
Nor any waters flow.

Francis Ledwidge

The Wind Among the Reeds

Mavrone, Mavrone! the wind among the reeds,
It calls and cries, and will not let me be;
And all its cry is of forgotten deeds
When men were loved of all the Daoine-sidhe.

O Sidhe that have forgotten how to love,
And Sidhe that have forgotten how to hate,
Asleep 'neath quicken boughs that no winds move,
Come back to us ere yet it be too late.

Pipe to us once again, lest we forget
What piping means, till all the Silver Spears
Be wild with gusty music, such as met
Carolan once, amid the dusty years.

Dance in your rings again: the yellow weeds
You used to ride so far, mount as of old—
Play hide and seek with winds among the reeds,
And pay your scores again with fairy gold.

Nora Hopper

To the Leanan Sidhe

Where is thy lovely perilous abode?
    In what strange phantom land
Glimmer the faerie turrets whereto rode
    The ill-starred poet band?

Say, in the Isle of Youth hast thou thy home,
    The sweetest singer there,
Stealing on wingéd steed across the foam
    Thorough the moonlit air,

And by the gloomy peak of Errigal,
    Haunted by storm and cloud,
Wing past, and to thy lover there let fall
    His singing robe . . . and shroud?

Or, where the mists of bluebell float beneath
    The red stems of the pine
And sunbeams strike through shadows, dost thou
        breathe
    The word that makes him thine?

Or, is thy palace entered through some cliff
    When radiant tides are full,
And round thy lover's wandering starlit skiff
    Coil in luxurious lull?

And, would he, entering on the brimming flood,
     See caverns vast in height,
And diamond columns crowned with leaf and bud,
     Glow in long lanes of light,

And there, the pearl of that great glittering shell,
     Trembling behold thee lone,
Now weaving in slow dance an awful spell,
     Now still upon thy throne?

Thy beauty!—ah, the eyes that pierce him through
     Then melt into a dream.
The voice that sings the mysteries of the blue
     And all that Be and Seem!

Thy lovely motions answering to the rime
     That ancient Nature sings,
That keeps the stars in cadence for all time
     And echoes through all things.

Whether he see thee thus, or in his dreams
     Thy light makes all lights dim:
An aching solitude from henceforth seems
     The world of men to him.

Thy luring song, above the sensuous roar,
   He follows with delight,
Shutting behind him Life's last gloomy door,
   And fares into the Night.

Thomas Boyd

The Others

From our hidden places
By a secret path
We troop in the moonlight
To the edge of the green rath.

There the night through
We take our pleasure
Dancing to such a measure
As earth never knew.

To song and dance
And lilt without a name
So sweetly breathéd
'Twould put a bird to shame.

And many a young maiden
Is there of mortal birth
Her young eyes laden
With dreams of earth.

And many a youth entrancéd
Moves slowly in the wildered round,
His brave lost feet enchanted
In the rhythm of elfin sound.

Music so forest wild
And piercing sweet would bring
Silence on blackbirds singing
Their best in the ear of Spring.

And now they pause in their dancing
And look with troubled eyes,
Earth's straying children
With sudden memory wise.

They pause, and their eyes in the moonlight
With faery wisdom cold,
Grow dim and a thought goes fluttering
In hearts no longer old.

And then the dream forsakes them
And sighing, they turn anew
As the whispering music takes them
To the dance of the elfin crew.

Oh, many a thrush and a blackbird
Would fall to the dewy ground
And pine away in silence
For envy of such a sound.

So the night through
In our sad pleasure
We dance to many a measure
That earth never knew.

Seumas O'Sullivan

CLXX

The Man Who Dreamed Of Faeryland

He stood among a crowd at Drumahair;
His heart hung all upon a silken dress,
And he had known at last some tenderness,
Before earth made of him her sleepy care;
But when a man poured fish into a pile,
It seemed they raised their little silver heads,
And sang how day a Druid twilight sheds

Upon a dim, green, well-beloved isle,
Where people love beside star-laden seas;
How Time may never mar their faery vows
Under the woven roofs of quicken boughs:
The singing shook him out of his new ease.

He wandered by the sands of Lisadill;
His mind ran all on money cares and fears,
And he had known at last some prudent years
Before they heaped his grave under the hill;
But while he passed before a plashy place,
A lug-worm with its grey and muddy mouth
Sang how somewhere to north or west or south
There dwelt a gay, exulting, gentle race;
And how beneath those three times blessed skies
A Danaan fruitage makes a shower of moons,
And as it falls awakens leafy tunes:
And at that singing he was no more wise.

He mused beside the well of Scanavin,
He mused upon his mockers: without fail
His sudden vengeance were a country tale,
Now that deep earth has drunk his body in;
But one small knot-grass growing by the pool
Told where, ah, little, all-unneeded voice!
Old Silence bids a lonely folk rejoice,

And chaplet their calm brows with leafage cool.
And how, when fades the sea-strewn rose of day,
A gentle feeling wraps them like a fleece,
And all their trouble dies into its peace:
The tale drove his fine angry mood away.

He slept under the hill of Lugnagall;
And might have known at last unhaunted sleep
Under that cold and vapour-turbaned steep,
Now that old earth had taken man and all:
Were not the worms that spired about his bones
A-telling with their low and reedy cry,
Of how God leans His hands out of the sky,
To bless that isle with honey in His tones;
That none may feel the power of squall and wave
And no one any leaf-crowned dancer miss
Until He burn up Nature with a kiss:
The man has found no comfort in the grave.

W. B. Yeats

The Poplars

As I went dreaming
By the grey poplar trees,
They bent down and whispered
Words like these.

"In a far country
There is a lonely glen,
Hushed with the footfall
Of shadowy men.

"Shadowy and silent,
And grey amongst the trees
That have long forgotten
The sound of the breeze.

"And one tall poplar
Grows in that land;
The chain of God's silence,
Held in his hand."

This I heard
As I went dreaming,
By the grey poplars
In the purple evening.

Seumas O'Sullivan

A Dream

I heard the dogs howl in the moonlight night;
I went to the window to see the sight;
All the Dead that ever I knew
Going one by one and two by two.

On they pass'd, and on they pass'd;
Townsfellows all, from first to last;
Born in the moonlight of the lane,
Quench'd in the heavy shadow again.

Schoolmates, marching as when we play'd
At soldiers once—but now more staid;
Those were the strangest sight to me
Who were drown'd, I knew, in the awful sea.

Straight and handsome folk; bent and weak too;
Some that I loved, and gasp'd to speak to;
Some but a day in their churchyard bed;
Some that I had not known were dead.

A long, long crowd—where each seem'd lonely,
Yet of them all there was one, one only,
Raised a head or look'd my way;
She linger'd a moment,—she might not stay.

How long since I saw that fair pale face!
Ah! Mother dear! might I only place
My head on thy breast, a moment to rest,
While thy hand on my tearful cheek were prest.

On, on, a moving bridge they made
Across the moon-stream, from shade to shade,
Young and old, women and men;
Many long-forgot, but remember'd then.

And first there came a bitter laughter;
A sound of tears the moment after;
And then a music so lofty and gay,
That every morning, day by day,
I strive to recall it if I may.

William Allingham

CLXXIII

The Maids of Elfin-Mere

When the spinning-room was here,
Came Three Damsels, clothed in white,
With their spindles every night;
One and two and three fair Maidens,
Spinning to a pulsing cadence,
Singing songs of Elfin-Mere;

Till the eleventh hour was toll'd,
Then departed through the wold.

Years ago, and years ago;
And the tall reeds sigh as the wind doth blow.

Three white Lilies, calm and clear,
And they were loved by every one;
Most of all, the Pastor's Son,
Listening to their gentle singing,
Felt his heart go from him, clinging
To these Maids of Elfin-Mere;
Sued each night to make them stay,
Sadden'd when they went away.

Years ago, and years ago;
And the tall reeds sigh as the wind doth blow.

Hands that shook with love and fear
Dared put back the village clock,—
Flew the spindle, turn'd the rock,
Flow'd the song with subtle rounding,
Till the false "eleven" was sounding;
Then these Maids of Elfin-Mere
Swiftly, softly left the room,
Like three doves on snowy plume.

Years ago, and years ago;
And the tall reeds sigh as the wind doth blow.

One that night who wander'd near
Heard lamentings by the shore,
Saw at dawn three stains of gore
In the waters fade and dwindle.
Never more with song and spindle
Saw we Maids of Elfin-Mere.
The Pastor's Son did pine and die;
Because true love should never lie.

> *Years ago, and years ago;*
> *And the tall reeds sigh as the wind doth blow.*

William Allingham

The King of Ireland's Son

Now all away to Tir na n'Og are many roads that
    run,
But he has ta'en the longest lane, the King of
    Ireland's son.

There's roads of hate, and roads of love, and
    many a middle way,
And castles keep the valleys deep where happy
    lovers stray—

Where Aongus goes there's many a rose burns red
    mid shadows dun,
No rose there is will draw his kiss, the King of
    Ireland's son.

And yonder, where the sun is high, Love laughs
    amid the hay,
But smile and sigh have passed him by, and never
    make delay.

And here (and O! the sun is low) they're glad for
    harvest won,
But naught he cares for wheat or tares, the King
    of Ireland's son!

And you have flung love's apple by, and I'm to
    pluck it yet:
But what are fruits of gramarye with Druid dews
    beset?

Oh, what are magic fruits to him who meets the
    Leanan-sidhe
Or hears athwart the distance dim Fionn's horn
    blow drowsily!
He follows on for ever when all your chase is done,
He follows after shadows, the King of Ireland's son.

Nora Hopper

The Host of the Air

O'Driscoll drove with a song
The wild duck and the drake
From the tall and the tufted reeds
Of the drear Hart Lake.

And he saw how the reeds grew dark
At the coming of night tide,
And dreamed of the long dim hair
Of Bridget his bride.

He heard while he sang and dreamed
A piper piping away,
And never was piping so sad,
And never was piping so gay.

And he saw young men and young girls
Who danced on a level place
And Bridget his bride among them,
With a sad and a gay face.

The dancers crowded about him,
And many a sweet thing said,
And a young man brought him red wine
And a young girl white bread.

But Bridget drew him by the sleeve,
Away from the merry bands,
To old men playing at cards
With a twinkling of ancient hands.

The bread and the wine had a doom,
For these were the host of the air;
He sat and played in a dream
Of her long dim hair.

He played with the merry old men
And thought not of evil chance,
Until one bore Bridget his bride
Away from the merry dance.

He bore her away in his arms,
The handsomest young man there,
And his neck and his breast and his arms
Were drowned in her long dim hair.

O'Driscoll scattered the cards
And out of his dream he awoke:
Old men and young men and young girls
Were gone like a drifting smoke;

But he heard high up in the air
A piper piping away,
And never was piping so sad,
And never was piping so gay.

W. B. Yeats

CLXXVI

The King's Son

Who rideth through the driving rain
At such a headlong speed?
Naked and pale he rides amain
Upon a naked steed.

Nor hollow nor height his going bars,
His wet steed shines like silk,
His head is golden to the stars
And his limbs are white as milk.

But, lo, he dwindles as a light
That lifts from a black mere,
And, as the fair youth wanes from sight,
The steed grows mightier.

What wizard by yon holy tree
   Mutters unto the sky
Where Macha's flame-tongued horses flee
   On hooves of thunder by?

Ah, 'tis not holy so to ban
   The youth of kingly seed:
Ah! woe, the wasting of a man
   Who changes to a steed.

Nightly upon the Plain of Kings
   When Macha's day is nigh
He gallops; and the dark wind brings
   His lonely human cry.

Thomas Boyd

CLXXVII

The Ghost

(TO OSBORN BERGIN)

Do not salute me, I am not your friend:
   He, that I image, is no more, is dead;
      I am his ghost.

If he had friends to grieve, if he had been
    In debt to them, how quickly they had heard
        That he was dead.

Ye think I loom not as an airy sprite,
    Nor as a phantom thinly shuddering
        To an old shape.

For all your senses are bewitched, are rapt away,
    And this, that ye salute, is but the ghost,
        The soulless one.

Ye greet that ye know not as it were known!
    Ye greet a goblin!—woe to him that shall
        Be haunted by me!

And still, and tho' I tell it still, ye say
    I am not dead—but I remember well
        The day I died.

—How should he mourn who, by an angel face,
    An angel vision, was translated
        Deathlessly?

—Or how outlive the loveliness, the wonder
    That slays all men? He saw that loveliness,
        He must be dead!

He did not fall in strife, nor lapse in woe
   —A very wildest, wildness of delight
     Hath killed him.

Not misery, not hate, could fetch him down!
   Not love, not love for her! terror it was
     That blinded him!

The terror of her beauty slew that man!
   All chill he comes, all ice of death he hears
     He is not dead!

He cannot tell those lips that did not dare
   To spy on them—but what his eye dared not
     His mind's eye saw. . . .

Remembering him, let no man brood upon
   The brow, the cheek—a wisp of goblin air
     That dolt will be. . . .

This death was painless, a death by her again
   Might well be woe! O God! forbid, forbid
     She raise her dead!

The Hound of Connacht once was that man called,
   His name was great, his fame was known
     Among the wise.

James Stephens
(After the Irish of Cú Chonnacht O Cléirigh)

271

The Gilly of Christ

I am the gilly of Christ,
The mate of Mary's Son;
I run the roads at seeding-time,
And when the harvest's done.

I sleep among the hills,
The heather is my bed;
I dip the termon-well for drink,
And pull the sloe for bread.

No eye has ever seen me,
But shepherds hear me pass,
Singing at fall of even
Along the shadowed grass.

The beetle is my bellman,
The meadow-fire my guide,
The bee and bat my ambling nags
When I have need to ride.

All know me only the Stranger,
Who sits on the Saxons' Height:
He burned the bacach's little house
On last St. Brigid's Night.

He sups off silver dishes,
And drinks in a golden horn,
But he will wake a wiser man
Upon the Judgment Morn.

I am the gilly of Christ,
The mate of Mary's Son;
I run the roads at seeding-time,
And when the harvest's done.

The seed I sow is lucky,
The corn I reap is red,
And whoso sings the "Gilly's Rann"
Will never cry for bread.

Joseph Campbell

CLXXIX

Ballad of Douglas Bridge

On Douglas Bridge I met a man
Who lived adjacent to Strabane,
    Before the English hung him high
For riding with O'Hanlon.

The eyes of him were just as fresh
As when they burned within the flesh;
　　　And his boot-legs were wide apart
From riding with O'Hanlon.

"God save you, Sir," I said with fear,
"You seem to be a stranger here."
　　　"Not I," said he, "nor any man
Who rides with Count O'Hanlon.

"I know each glen from North Tyrone
To Monaghan, and I've been known
　　　By every clan and parish, since
I rode with Count O'Hanlon.

"Before that time," said he to me,
"My fathers owned the land you see;
　　　But they are now among the moors
A-riding with O'Hanlon.

"Before that time," said he with pride,
"My fathers rode where now they ride
　　　As Rapparees, before the time
Of trouble and O'Hanlon.

"Good night to you, and God be with
The tellers of the tale and myth,
    For they are of the spirit-stuff
That rides with Count O'Hanlon."

"Good night to you," said I, "and God
Be with the chargers, fairy-shod,
    That bear the Ulster heroes forth
To ride with Count O'Hanlon."

On Douglas Bridge we parted, but
The Gap o' Dreams is never shut
    To one whose saddled soul to-night
Rides out with Count O'Hanlon.

Francis Carlin

CLXXX
The Plougher

Sunset and silence! A man: around him earth
    savage, earth broken;
Beside him two horses—a plough!

Earth savage, earth broken, the brutes, the dawn
      man there in the sunset,
And the Plough that is twin to the Sword, that is
      founder of cities!

"Brute-tamer, plough-maker, earth-breaker! Can'st
      hear?
  There are ages between us.
Is it praying you are as you stand there alone in
      the sunset?

"Surely our sky-born gods can be naught to you,
      earth child and earth master?
Surely your thoughts are of Pan, or of Wotan, or
      Dana?

"Yet, why give thought to the gods? Has Pan led
      your brutes where they stumble?
Has Dana numbed pain of the child-bed, or
      Wotan put hands to your plough?

"What matter your foolish reply! O, man, standing
      lone and bowed earthward,
Your task is a day near its close. Give thanks to
      the night-giving God."

*   *   *   *   *

Slowly the darkness falls, the broken lands blend
    with the savage;
The brute-tamer stands by the brutes, a head's
    breadth only above them.

A head's breadth? Ay, but therein is hell's depth,
    and the height up to heaven,
And the thrones of the gods and their halls, their
    chariots, purples, and splendours.

Padraic Colum

CLXXXI

The Dancer

The tall dancer dances
With slowly-taken breath:
In his feet music,
And on his face death.

His face is a mask,
It is so still and white:
His withered eyes shut,
Unmindful of light.

The old fiddler fiddles
The merry "*Silver Tip*"
With softly-beating foot
And laughing eye and lip.

And round the dark walls
The people sit and stand,
Praising the art
Of the dancer of the land.

But he dances there
As if his kin were dead:
Clay in his thoughts,
And lightning in his tread.

Joseph Campbell

CLXXXII

The Old Woman

As a white candle
In a holy place,
So is the beauty
Of an agèd face.

As the spent radiance
Of the winter sun,
So is a woman
With her travail done.

Her brood gone from her,
And her thoughts as still
As the waters
Under a ruined mill.

Joseph Campbell

A Poor Scholar of the Forties

My eyelids red and heavy are,
With bending o'er the smould'ring peat.
I know the Aeneid now by heart,
My Virgil read in cold and heat,
In loneliness and hunger smart.
    And I know Homer, too, I ween,
    As Munster poets know Ossian.

And I must walk this road that winds
'Twixt bog and bog, while east there lies
A city with its men and books,
With treasures open to the wise,

Heart-words from equals, comrade-looks;
    Down here they have but tale and song
    They talk Repeal the whole night long.

"You teach Greek verbs and Latin nouns,"
The dreamer of Young Ireland said.
"You do not hear the muffled call,
The sword being forged, the far-off tread
Of hosts to meet as Gael and Gall—
    What good to us your wisdom store,
    Your Latin verse, your Grecian lore?"

And what to me is Gael or Gall?
Less than the Latin or the Greek.
I teach these by the dim rush-light,
In smoky cabins night and week.
But what avail my teaching slight?
    Years hence, in rustic speech, a phrase,
    As in wild earth a Grecian vase!

                                    Padraic Colum

CLXXXIV

"Ballyvourney"

He came from Ballyvourney and we called him
    "Ballyvourney,"
  The sweetest name in Erinn that we know,
And they tell me he has taken now the last, the
    last long Journey,
  And it's young he is, it's young he is so very far
    to go.

He came from Ballyvourney, from the town set in
    the morning
  That has caught the lights, the lights of Dawn,
    we have waited for so long,
And he was Ballyvourney, the Child of Erinn's
    morning
  In his hope that shone before him, in his speech
    more sweet than song.

Where are you, Ballyvourney? God is good and
    will be giving
  Their own heaven, as they wish it, to the Gael:
In an island like our island there in joy you will be
    living
  Where the simple joys you loved will never fail.

There you strike the golden ball and there you will
    be dancing.
  Who but you could foot it well? I have seen you
    many a time;
And there you rest by shining trees, where lights
    of heaven are glancing,
  Listening to the holy birds that sing the hours
    in chime.

Before our eyes, just like a flower, we saw your life
    unfolding
  As day by day you grew in bloom of early
    manhood's grace:
Ah, Death! to pluck the flower and to snatch from
    our beholding
  The head of rippled gold and the happy
    morning face.

Thomas Boyd

Nelson Street

There is hardly a mouthful of air
In the room where the breakfast is set,
For the blind is still down though it's late,
And the curtains are redolent yet
Of tobacco smoke, stale from last night.
There's the little bronze teapot, and there
The eggs on the blue willow-plate,
And the sleepy canary, a hen,
Starts faintly her chirruping tweet
And I know, could she speak, she would say,
"Hullo there—what's wrong with the light,
Draw the blind up, let's look at the day."
I see that it's Monday again,
For the man with the organ is there;
Every Monday he comes to the street
(Lest I, or the bird there, should miss
Our count of monotonous days)
With his reed-organ, wheezy and sweet,
And stands by the window and plays
"There's a Land that is Fairer than This."

Seumas O'Sullivan

The Woman of Three Cows

O Woman of Three Cows, *agra!* don't let your
    tongue thus rattle!
O, don't be saucy, don't be stiff, because you may
    have cattle.
I have seen—and, here's my hand to you, I only
    say what's true—
A many a one with twice your stock not half so
    proud as you.

Good luck to you, don't scorn the poor, and don't
    be their despiser,
For worldly wealth soon melts away, and cheats
    the very miser,
And Death soon strips the proudest wreath from
    haughty human brows;
Then don't be stiff, and don't be proud, good
    Woman of Three Cows!

See where Momonia's heroes lie, proud Owen
    More's descendants,
'Tis they that won the glorious name, and had the
    grand attendants!

If *they* were forced to bow to Fate, as every mortal
    bows,
Can *you* be proud, can *you* be stiff, my Woman of
    Three Cows!

The brave sons of the Lord of Clare, they left the
    land to mourning;
Mavrone! for they were banished, with no hope of
    their returning—
Who knows in what abodes of want those youths
    were driven to house?
Yet *you* can give yourself these airs, O Woman of
    Three Cows!

O, think of Donnell of the Ships, the Chief whom
    nothing daunted—
See how he fell in distant Spain, unchronicled,
    unchanted!
He sleeps, the great O'Sullivan, where thunder
    cannot rouse—
Then ask yourself, should *you* be proud, good
    Woman of Three Cows!

O'Ruark, Maguire, those souls of fire, whose
    names are shrined in story—
Think how their high achievements once made
    Erin's highest glory—

Yet now their bones lie mouldering under weeds
    and cypress boughs,
And so, for all your pride, will yours, O Woman of
    Three Cows!

Your neighbour's poor, and you, it seems, are big
    with vain ideas,
Because, *inagh*, you've got three cows—one more,
    I see, than *she* has.
That tongue of yours wags more at times than
    Charity allows,
But if you're strong, be merciful, great Woman of
    Three Cows!

THE SUMMING UP

Now, there you go! You still, of course, keep up
    your scornful bearing,
And I'm too poor to hinder you; but, by the cloak
    I'm wearing,
If I had but *four* cows myself, even though you
    were my spouse,
I'd thwack you well to cure your pride, my Woman
    of Three Cows!

James Clarence Mangan
(From the Irish)

Beg-Innish

Bring Kateen-beug and Maurya Jude
To dance in Beg-Innish,
And when the lads (they're in Dunquin)
Have sold their crabs and fish,
Wave fawny shawls and call them in,
And call the little girls who spin,
And seven weavers from Dunquin,
To dance in Beg-Innish.

I'll play you jigs, and Maurice Kean,
Where nets are laid to dry,
I've silken strings would draw a dance
From girls are lame or shy;
Four strings I've brought from Spain and France
To make your long men skip and prance,
Till stars look out to see the dance
Where nets are laid to dry.

We'll have no priest or peeler in
To dance in Beg-Innish;
But we'll have drink from M'riarty Jim
Rowed round while gannets fish,

A keg with porter to the brim,
That every lad may have his whim,
Till we up sails with M'riarty Jim
And sail from Beg-Innish.

J. M. Synge

CLXXXVIII

Galway Races

It's there you'll see confectioners with sugar sticks
    and dainties,
The lozenges and oranges, lemonade and the
    raisins;
The gingerbread and spices to accommodate the
    ladies,
And a big crubeen for threepence to be picking
    while you're able.

It's there you'll see the gamblers, the thimbles and
    the garters,
And the sporting Wheel of Fortune with the four
    and twenty quarters.
There was others without scruple pelting wattles
    at poor Maggy,

288

And her father well contented and he looking at
　　his daughter.

It's there you'll see the pipers and fiddlers
　　competing,
And the nimble-footed dancers and they tripping
　　on the daisies.
There was others crying segars and lights, and
　　bills of all the races,
With the colour of the jockeys, the prize and
　　horses' ages.

It's there you'd see the jockeys and they mounted
　　on most stately,
The pink and blue, the red and green, the
　　Emblem of our nation.
When the bell was rung for starting, the horses
　　seemed impatient,
Though they never stood on ground, their speed
　　was so amazing.

There was half a million people there of all
　　denominations,
The Catholic, the Protestant, the Jew and
　　Prespetarian.

There was yet no animosity, no matter what
    persuasion,
But *failte* and hospitality, inducing fresh
    acquaintance.

Anonymous

CLXXXIX
The Rakes Of Mallow

Beauing, belling, dancing, drinking,
Breaking windows, damning, sinking,
Ever raking, never thinking,
    Live the rakes of Mallow.

Spending faster than it comes,
Beating waiters, bailiffs, duns,
Bacchus' true-begotten sons,
    Live the rakes of Mallow.

One, time naught but claret drinking,
Then like politicians thinking
To raise the sinking funds when sinking,
    Live the rakes of Mallow.

When at home with dadda dying
Still for Mallow water crying;

But where there's good claret plying,
　　　Live the rakes of Mallow.

Living short, but merry lives;
Going where the devil drives;
Having sweethearts, but no wives,
　　　Live the rakes of Mallow.

Racking tenants, stewards teasing,
Swiftly spending, slowly raising,
Wishing to spend all their lives in
　　　Raking as in Mallow.

Then to end this raking life,
They get sober, take a wife,
Ever after live in strife,
　　　And wish again for Mallow.

Anonymous

CXC

Elegy on the Death of a Mad Dog

Good people all, of every sort,
　　Give ear unto my song;
And if you find it wond'rous short,
　　It cannot hold you long.

In Islington there was a man,
 Of whom the world might say,
That still a godly race he ran,
 Whene'er he went to pray.

A kind and gentle heart he had,
 To comfort friends and foes;
The naked every day he clad,
 When he put on his clothes.

And in that town a dog was found,
 As many dogs there be,
Both mongrel, puppy, whelp, and hound,
 And curs of low degree.

This dog and man at first were friends;
 But when a pique began,
The dog, to gain some private ends,
 Went mad and bit the man.

Around from all the neighbouring streets
 The wond'ring neighbours ran,
And swore the dog had lost his wits,
 To bite so good a man.

The wound it seem'd both sore and sad
    To every Christian eye;
And while they swore the dog was mad,
    They swore the man would die.

But soon a wonder came to light,
    That show'd the rogues they lied:
The man recover'd of the bite,
    The dog it was that died.

Oliver Goldsmith

CXCI

Mrs. Frances Harris's Petition

To their Excellencies the Lords Justices of Ireland,
The humble petition of Frances Harris,
Who must starve and die a maid if it miscarries;
Humbly sheweth, that I went to warm myself in
    Lady Betty's chamber, because I was cold;
And I had in a purse seven pounds, four shillings,
    and sixpence (besides farthings) in money
    and gold;
So because I had been buying things for my lady
    last night,

I was resolved to tell my money, to see if it was
    right.
Now, you must know, because my trunk has a very
    bad lock,
Therefore all the money I have, which, God
    knows, is a very small stock,
I keep it in my pocket, ty'd about my middle, next
    my smock.
So when I went to put up my purse, as God
    would have it, my smock was unript,
And instead of putting it into my pocket, down it
    slipt;
Then the bell rung, and I went down to put my
    lady to bed;
And, God knows I thought my money was as safe
    as my maidenhead.
So, when I came up again, I found my pocket feel
    very light;
But when I search'd, and miss'd my purse, Lord! I
    thought I should have sunk outright,
"Lord! madam," says Mary, "how d'ye do?"—
    "Indeed," says I, "never worse:
But pray, Mary, can you tell what I have done
    with my purse?"
"Lord help me!" says Mary, "I never stirr'd out of
    this place!"

"Nay," said I, "I had it in Lady Betty's chamber, that's a plain case."

So Mary got me to bed, and covered me up warm:

However, she stole away my garters, that I might do myself no harm.

So I tumbled and toss'd all night, as you may very well think,

But hardly ever set my eyes together, or slept a wink.

So I was a-dream'd, methought, that I went and searched the folks round,

And in a corner of Mrs. Duke's box, ty'd in a rag, the money was found,

So next morning we told Whittle, and he fell a swearing:

Then my Dame Wadgar came, and she, you know, is thick of hearing.

"Dame," said I, as loud as I could bawl, "do you know what a loss I have had?"

"Nay," says she, "my Lord Colway's folks are all very sad:

For my Lord Dromedary comes a Tuesday without fail."

"Pugh!" said I, "but that's not the business that I ail."

Says Carey, says he, "I have been a servant this
    five-and-twenty years come spring,
And in all the places I lived I never heard of such
    a thing."
"Yes," says the steward, "I remember when I was
    at my Lord Shrewsbury's,
Such a thing as this happen'd, just about the time
    of *gooseberries*."
So I went to the party suspected, and I found her
    full of grief:
(Now you must know, of all the things in the
    world I hate a thief:)
However, I was resolved to bring the discourse
    slily about:
"Mrs. Duke," said I, "here's an ugly accident has
    happened out:
'Tis not that I value the money three skips of a
    louse:
But the thing I stand upon is the credit of the
    house.
'Tis true, seven pounds, four shillings, and
    sixpence makes a great hole in my wages:
Besides, as they say, service is no inheritance in
    these ages.
Now, Mrs. Duke, you know, and everybody
    understands,

That though 'tis hard to judge, yet money can't go
without hands."

"The *devil* take me!" said she, (blessing herself,)
"if ever I saw't!"

So she roar'd like a bedlam, as tho' I had call'd
her all to naught.

So, you know, what could I say to her any more?

I e'en left her, and came away as wise as I was
before.

Well: but then they would have had me gone to
the cunning man:

"No," said I, "'tis the same thing, the
CHAPLAIN will be here anon."

So the Chaplain came in. Now the servants say he
is my sweetheart,

Because he's always in my chamber, and I always
take his part.

So, as the *devil* would have it, before I was aware,
out I blunder'd,

"*Parson*," said I, "can you cast a *nativity*, when a
body's plunder'd?"

(Now you must know, he hates to be called
Parson, like the *devil!*)

"Truly," says he, "Mrs. Nab, it might become you
to be more civil;

If your money be gone, as a learned *Divine* says,
    d'ye see,
You are no *text* for my handling; so take that from
    me:
I was never taken for a *Conjuror* before, I'd have
    you to know."
"Lord!" said I, "don't be angry, I am sure I never
    thought you so;
You know I honour the cloth, I design to be a
    Parson's wife;
I never took one in *your coat* for a conjuror in all
    my life."
With that he twisted his girdle at me like a rope,
    as who should say,
"Now you may go hang yourself for me!" and so
    went away.
Well: I thought I should have swoon'd. "Lord!"
    said I, "what shall I do?
I have lost my money, and shall lose my true love
    too!"
Then my lord call'd me: "Harry," said my lord,
    "don't cry;
I'll give you something toward thy loss": "And,"
    says my lady, "so will I."
"Oh! but," said I, "what if, after all, the Chaplain
    won't come to?"

For that, he said (an't please your Excellencies), I
    must petition you.
The premises tenderly consider'd, I desire your
    Excellencies' protection,
And that I may have a share in next Sunday's
    collection;
And, over and above, that I may have your
    Excellencies' letter,
With an order for the Chaplain aforesaid, or
    instead of him, a better:
And then your poor petitioner, both night and day,
Or the Chaplain (for 'tis his *trade*,) as in duty
    bound, shall ever *pray*.

Jonathan Swift

CXCII

The Village Preacher

Near yonder copse, where once the garden smil'd,
And still where many a garden flower grows wild;
There, where a few torn shrubs the place disclose,
The village preacher's modest mansion rose.
A man he was to all the country dear,
And passing rich with forty pounds a year;
Remote from towns he ran his godly race,

Nor e'er had chang'd, nor wished to change his
    place;
Unpractis'd he to fawn, or seek for power,
By doctrines fashion'd to the varying hour;
For other aims his heart had learn'd to prize,
More skill'd to raise the wretched than to rise.
His house was known to all the vagrant train,
He chid their wand'rings, but relieved their pain;
The long-remember'd beggar was his guest,
Whose beard descending swept his aged breast.
The ruin'd spendthrift, now no longer proud,
Claim'd kindred there, and had his claims allow'd;
The broken soldier, kindly bade to stay,
Sat by his fire, and talk'd the night away;
Wept o'er his wounds, or, tales of sorrow done,
Shoulder'd his crutch, and show'd how fields were
    won.
Pleas'd with his guests, the good man learned to
    glow,
And quite forgot their vices in their woe;
Careless their merits or their faults to scan,
His pity gave ere charity began.

Thus to relieve the wretched was his pride,
And e'en his failings lean'd to Virtue's side;
But in his duty prompt at every call,

He watch'd and wept, he pray'd and felt, for all;
And, as a bird each fond endearment tries
To tempt its new-fledg'd offspring to the skies,
He tried each art, reprov'd each dull delay,
Allur'd to brighter worlds, and led the way.

Oliver Goldsmith

CXCIII

On a Curate's Complaint of Hard Duty

I march'd three miles through scorching sand,
With zeal in heart, and notes in hand;
I rode four more to Great St. Mary,
Using four legs, when two were weary:
To three fair virgins I did tie men,
In the close bands of pleasing Hymen;
I dipp'd two babes in holy water,
And purified their mother after.
Within an hour and eke a half,
I preach'd three congregations deaf;
Where, thundering out, with lungs long-winded,
I chopp'd so fast, that few there minded.
My emblem, the laborious sun,
Saw all these mighty labours done

Before one race of his was run.
All this perform'd by Robert Hewit:
What mortal else could e'er go through it!

Jonathan Swift

The Groves of Blarney

The groves of Blarney
They look so charming,
Down by the purling
   Of sweet, silent brooks,
Being banked with posies
That spontaneous grow there,
Planted in order
   By the sweet "Rock Close."
'Tis there the daisy
And the sweet carnation,
The blooming pink
   And the rose so fair.
The daffodowndilly,
Likewise the lily,
All flowers that scent
   The sweet, fragrant air.

'Tis Lady Jeffers
That owns this station;
Like Alexander,
    Or Queen Helen fair,
There's no commander
In all the nation,
For emulation,
    Can with her compare.
Such walls surround her,
That no nine-pounder
Could dare to plunder
    Her place of strength;
But Oliver Cromwell
Her he did pommell,
And made a breach
    In her battlement.

There's gravel walks there
For speculation
And conversation
    In sweet solitude.
'Tis there the lover
May hear the dove, or
The gentle plover
    In the afternoon;
And if a lady

Would be so engaging
As to walk alone in
    Those shady bowers,
'Tis there the courtier
He may transport her
Into some fort, or
    All underground.

For 'tis there's a cave where
No daylight enters,
But cats and badgers
    Are for ever bred;
Being mossed by nature,
That makes it sweeter
Than a coach-and-six or
    A feather bed.
'Tis there the lake is,
Well stored with perches,
And comely eels in
    The verdant mud;
Besides the leeches,
And groves of beeches,
Standing in order
    For to guard the flood.

There's statues gracing
This noble place in—
All heathen gods
    And nymphs so fair;
Bold Neptune, Plutarch,
And Nicodemus,
All standing naked
    In the open air!
So now to finish
This brave narration,
Which my poor genii
    Could not entwine;
But were I Homer,
Or Nebuchadnezzar,
'Tis in every feature
    I would make it shine.

Richard Alfred Milliken

CXCV

The Night Before Larry was Stretched

The night before Larry was stretched,
    The boys they all paid him a visit;
A bait in their sacks, too, they fetched;
    They sweated their duds till they riz it;

For Larry was ever the lad,
When a boy was condemned to the squeezer,
Would fence all the duds that he had
To help a poor friend to a sneezer,
And warm his gob 'fore he died.

The boys they came crowding in fast,
They drew all their stools round about him,
Six glims round his trap-case were placed,
He couldn't be well waked without 'em.
When one of us asked could he die
Without having truly repented,
Says Larry, "That's all in my eye,
And first by the clargy invented,
To get a fat bit for themselves."

"I'm sorry, dear Larry," says I,
"To see you in this situation;
And, blister my limbs if I lie,
I'd as lieve it had been my own station."
"Ochone! it's all over," says he,
"For the neck-cloth I'll be forced to put on,
And by this time to-morrow you'll see
Your poor Larry as dead as a mutton,
Because, why, his courage was good.

"And I'll be cut up like a pie,
And my nob from my body be parted."
"You're in the wrong box, then," says I,
"For blast me if they're so hard-hearted;
A chalk on the back of your neck
Is all that Jack Ketch dares to give you;
Then mind not such trifles a feck,
For why should the likes of them grieve you?
And now, boys, come tip us the deck."

The cards being called for, they played,
Till Larry found one of them cheated;
A dart at his napper he made
(The boy being easily heated);
"O, by the hokey, you thief,
I'll scuttle your nob with my daddle!
You cheat me because I'm in grief,
But soon I'll demolish your noddle,
And leave you your claret to drink."

Then the clergy came in with his book,
He spoke him so smooth and so civil;
Larry tipped him a Kilmainham look,
And pitched his big wig to the devil;
Then sighing, he threw back his head,
To get a sweet drop of the bottle,
And pitiful sighing, he said:

"Oh, the hemp will be soon round my throttle,
And choke my poor windpipe to death."

"Though sure it's the best way to die,
O! the devil a better a-livin'!
For when the gallows is high
Your journey is shorter to heaven:"
But what harasses Larry the most,
And makes his poor soul melancholy,
Is that he thinks of the time when his ghost
Will come in a sheet to sweet Molly;
"O, sure it will kill her alive!"

So moving these last words he spoke,
We all vented our tears in a shower;
For my part, I thought my heart broke,
To see him cut down like a flower.
On his travels we watched him next day;
O! the throttler, I thought I could kill him;
But Larry not one word did say,
Nor changed till he came to "King William,"
Then, *musha*, his colour grew white.

When we came to the numbing chit,
He was tucked up so neat and so pretty,
The rumbler jogged off from his feet,
And he died with his face to the city;

He kicked, too—but that was all pride,
For soon you might see 'twas all over;
Soon after the noose was untied,
And at darkee we waked him in clover,
And sent him to take a ground sweat.

Anonymous

Johnny, I Hardly Knew Ye

While going the road to sweet Athy,
    Hurroo! hurroo!
While going the road to sweet Athy,
    Hurroo! hurroo!
While going the road to sweet Athy,
A stick in my hand and a drop in my eye,
A doleful damsel I heard cry;—
    "Och, Johnny, I hardly knew ye!
With drums and guns and guns and drums,
    The enemy nearly slew ye,
    My darling dear, you look so queer,
    Och, Johnny, I hardly knew ye!

"Where are your eyes that looked so mild?
    Hurroo! hurroo!

Where are your eyes that looked so mild?
     Hurroo! hurroo!
Where are your eyes that looked so mild
When my poor heart you first beguiled?
Why did you run from me and the child?
     Och, Johnny, I hardly knew ye!
With drums, etc.

"Where are the legs with which you run?
     Hurroo! hurroo!
Where are the legs with which you run?
     Hurroo! hurroo!
Where are the legs with which you run,
When you went to carry a gun?—
Indeed, your dancing days are done!
     Och, Johnny, I hardly knew ye!
With drums, etc.

"It grieved my heart to see you sail,
     Hurroo! hurroo!
It grieved my heart to see you sail,
     Hurroo! hurroo!
It grieved my heart to see you sail,
Though from my heart you took leg bail,—
Like a cod you're doubled up head and tail.
     Och, Johnny, I hardly knew ye!
With drums, etc.

"You haven't an arm and you haven't a leg,
      Hurroo! hurroo!
You haven't an arm and you haven't a leg,
      Hurroo! hurroo!
You haven't an arm and you haven't a leg,
You're an eyeless, noseless, chickenless egg;
You'll have to be put in a bowl to beg;
      Och, Johnny, I hardly knew ye!
With drums, etc.

"I'm happy for to see you home,
      Hurroo! hurroo!
I'm happy for to see you home,
      Hurroo! hurroo!
I'm happy for to see you home,
All from the island of Sulloon,
So low in flesh, so high in bone,
      Och, Johnny, I hardly knew ye!
With drums, etc.

"But sad as it is to see you so,
      Hurroo! hurroo!
But sad as it is to see you so,
      Hurroo! hurroo!
But sad as it is to see you so,
And to think of you now as an object of woe,

Your Peggy'll still keep ye on as her beau;
    Och, Johnny, I hardly knew ye!
With drums and guns and guns and drums,
    The enemy nearly slew ye,
    My darling dear, you look so queer,
    Och, Johnny, I hardly knew ye!"

Anonymous

CXCVII

The Burial of Sir John Moore

Not a drum was heard, not a funeral note,
    As his corse to the ramparts we hurried;
Not a soldier discharged his farewell shot
    O'er the grave where our hero we buried.

We buried him darkly, at dead of night,
    The sods with our bayonets turning,
By the struggling moonbeam's misty light,
    And the lantern dimly burning.

No useless coffin enclosed his breast,
    Not in sheet nor in shroud we wound him;
But he lay like a warrior taking his rest,
    With his martial cloak around him.

Few and short were the prayers we said,
  And we spoke not a word of sorrow;
But we steadfastly gazed on the face that was dead,
  And we bitterly thought of the morrow.

We thought as we hollowed his narrow bed,
  And smoothed down his lonely pillow,
That the foe and the stranger would tread o'er his
      head,
  And we far away on the billow!

Lightly they'll talk of the spirit that's gone,
  And o'er his cold ashes upbraid him,—
But little he'll reck if they let him sleep on
  In the grave where a Briton has laid him.

But half of our heavy task was done,
  When the clock struck the hour for retiring,
And we heard the distant and random gun
  That the foe was sullenly firing.

Slowly and sadly we laid him down,
  From the field of his fame fresh and gory;
We carved not a line, and we raised not a stone—
  But we left him alone in his glory!

Charles Wolfe

By the Statue of King Charles
at Charing Cross

Sombre and rich, the skies;
Great glooms, and starry plains.
Gently the night wind sighs;
Else a vast silence reigns.

The splendid silence clings
Around me: and around
The saddest of all kings
Crowned, and again discrowned.

Comely and calm, he rides
Hard by his own Whitehall:
Only the night wind glides:
No crowds, nor rebels, brawl.

Gone, too, his Court: and yet.
The stars his courtiers are:
Stars in their stations set;
And every wandering star.

Alone he rides, alone,
The fair and fatal king:
Dark night is all his own,
That strange and solemn thing.

Which are more full of fate:
The stars; or those sad eyes?
Which are more still and great:
Those brows; or the dark skies?

Although his whole heart yearn
In passionate tragedy:
Never was face so stern
With sweet austerity.

Vanquished in life, his death
By beauty made amends:
The passing of his breath
Won his defeated ends.

Brief life, and hapless? Nay:
Through death, life grew sublime.
Speak after sentence? Yea:
And to the end of time.

Armoured he rides, his head
Bare to the stars of doom:
He triumphs now, the dead,
Beholding London's gloom.

Our wearier spirit faints,
Vexed in the world's employ:
His soul was of the saints;
And art to him was joy.

King, tried in fires of woe!
Men hunger for thy grace:
And through the night I go,
Loving thy mournful face.

Yet, when the city sleeps;
When all the cries are still:
The stars and heavenly deeps
Work out a perfect will.

Lionel Johnson

CXCIX

The Monk

I go with silent feet and slow
As all my black-robed brothers go;
I dig a while and read and pray,
So portion out my quiet day
Until the evening time, and then
Work at my book with cunning pen.
If she would turn to me a while,

If she would turn to me and smile,
My book would be no more to me
Than some forgotten phantasy,
And God no more unto my mind
Than a dead leaf upon the wind.

Seumas O'Sullivan

CC

Enemies

... And you, O most of all
I hate, whose wisdom is
But to be cynical,—
The knave's analysis.
You who have never known
The heart set wild with a word,
Or seen the swallows blown
Northward when spring has stirred
The wing's rebellion.

I wonder if you found,
Beaten with wind and sun,
A swallow on the ground,
Would even a moment's thought

Trouble you with a fleet
Pain, that such daring brought
Such passionate defeat.

R. N. D. Wilson

I Am Raftery

I am Raftery the Poet
  Full of hope and love,
With eyes that have no light,
  With gentleness that has no misery.

Going west upon my pilgrimage
  By the light of my heart,
Feeble and tired
  To the end of my road.

Behold me now,
  And my face to the wall,
A-playing music
  Unto empty pockets.

Douglas Hyde
(From the Irish of Raftery)

Warning And Reply

In the earth—the earth—thou shalt be laid,
   A grey stone standing over thee;
Black mould beneath thee spread,
   And black mould to cover thee.

"Well—there is rest there,
   So fast come thy prophecy;
The time when my sunny hair
   Shall with grass roots entwined be."

But cold—cold is that resting-place,
   Shut out from joy and liberty,
And all who loved thy living face
   Will shrink from it shudderingly.

"Not so. *Here* the world is chill,
   And sworn friends fall from me;
But *there*—they will own me still,
   And prize my memory."

Farewell, then, all that love,
   All that deep sympathy:
Sleep on: Heaven laughs above,
   Earth never misses thee.

Turf-sod and tombstone drear
   Part human company;
One heart breaks only—here,
   But that heart was worthy thee!

Emily Brontë

The Nameless One

Roll forth, my song, like the rushing river,
   That sweeps along to the mighty sea;
God will inspire me while I deliver
       My soul of thee!

Tell thou the world, when my bones lie whitening
   Amid the last homes of youth and eld,
That there was once one whose veins ran lightning
       No eye beheld.

Tell how his boyhood was one drear night-hour,
   How shone for *him*, through his griefs and
     gloom,
No star of all heaven sends to light our
       Path to the tomb.

Roll on, my song, and to after ages
  Tell how, disdaining all earth can give,
He would have taught men, from wisdom's pages,
          The way to live.

And tell how trampled, derided, hated,
  And worn by weakness, disease, and wrong,
He fled for shelter to God, who mated
          His soul with song—

With song which alway, sublime or vapid,
  Flowed like a rill in the morning beam,
Perchance not deep, but intense and rapid—
          A mountain stream.

Tell how this Nameless, condemned for years long
  To herd with demons from hell beneath,
Saw things that made him, with groans and tears,
    long
          For even death.

Go on to tell how, with genius wasted,
  Betrayed in friendship, befooled in love,
With spirit shipwrecked, and young hopes blasted,
          He still, still strove.

Till, spent with toil, dreeing death for others,
  And some whose hands should have wrought
    for *him*
(If children live not for sires and mothers),
        His mind grew dim.

And he fell far through that pit abysmal
  The gulf and grave of Maginn and Burns,
And pawned his soul for the devil's dismal
        Stock of returns.

But yet redeemed it in days of darkness
  And shapes and signs of the final wrath,
When death, in hideous and ghastly starkness,
        Stood on his path.

And tell how, now, amid wreck and sorrow
  And want, and sickness, and houseless nights
He bides in calmness the silent morrow,
        That no ray lights.

And lives he still, then? Yes! Old and hoary
  At thirty-nine, from despair and woe,
He lives enduring what future story
        Will never know.

Him grant a grave to, ye pitying noble,
   Deep in your bosoms! There let him dwell!
He, too, had tears for all souls in trouble,
            Here, and in hell.

James Clarence Mangan

The Dark Angel

Dark Angel, with thine aching lust
To rid the world of penitence:
Malicious Angel, who still dost
My soul such subtile violence!

Because of thee, no thought, no thing
Abides for me undesecrate:
Dark Angel, ever on the wing,
Who never reachest me too late!

When music sounds, then changest thou
Its silvery to a sultry fire:
Nor will thine envious heart allow
Delight untortured by desire

Through thee, the gracious Muses turn
To Furies, O mine Enemy!
And all the things of beauty burn
With flames of evil ecstasy.

Because of thee, the land of dreams
Becomes a gathering-place of fears:
Until tormented slumber seems
One vehemence of useless tears.

When sunlight glows upon the flowers,
Or ripples down the dancing sea:
Thou, with thy troop of passionate powers,
Beleaguerest, bewilderest me.

Within the breath of autumn woods,
Within the winter silences:
Thy venomous spirit stirs and broods,
O Master of impieties!

The ardour of red flame is thine,
And thine the steely soul of ice:
Thou poisonest the fair design
Of nature, with unfair device.

Apples of ashes, golden bright;
Waters of bitterness, how sweet!
O banquet of a foul delight,
Prepared by thee, dark Paraclete.

Thou art the whisper in the gloom,
The hinting tone, the haunting laugh:
Thou art the adorner of my tomb,
The minstrel of mine epitaph.

I fight thee, in the Holy Name!
Yet, what thou dost, is what God saith:
Tempter! should I escape thy flame,
Thou wilt have helped my soul from Death:

The second Death, that never dies,
That cannot die, when time is dead:
Live Death, wherein the lost soul cries,
Eternally uncomforted.

Dark Angel, with thine aching lust!
Of two defeats, of two despairs:
Less dread, a change to drifting dust,
Than thine eternity of cares.

Do what thou wilt, thou shalt not so,
Dark Angel! triumph over me:
Lonely, unto the Lone I go;
Divine, to the Divinity.

Lionel Johnson

CCV

Helas!

To drift with every passion till my soul
Is a stringed lute on which all winds can play,
Is it for this that I have given away
Mine ancient wisdom, and austere control?
Methinks my life is a twice-written scroll
Scrawled over on some boyish holiday
With idle songs for pipe and virelay,
Which do but mar the secret of the whole.
Surely there was a time I might have trod
The sunlit heights, and from life's dissonance
Struck one clear chord to reach the ears of God:
Is that time dead? lo! with a little rod
I did but touch the honey of romance—
And must I lose a soul's inheritance?

Oscar Wilde

Mystic and Cavalier

Go from me: I am one of those who fall.
What! hath no cold wind swept your heart at all,
In my sad company? Before the end,
        Go from me, dear my friend!

Yours are the victories of light: your feet
Rest from good toil, where rest is brave and sweet.
But after warfare in a mourning gloom,
        I rest in clouds of doom.

Have you not read so, looking in these eyes?
Is it the common light of the pure skies,
Lights up their shadowy depths? The end is set:
        Though the end be not yet.

When gracious music stirs, and all is bright,
And beauty triumphs through a courtly night;
When I too joy, a man like other men:
        Yet, am I like them, then?

And in the battle, when the horsemen sweep
Against a thousand deaths, and fall on sleep:
Who ever sought that sudden calm, if I
        Sought not? Yet, could not die.

Seek with thine eyes to pierce this crystal sphere:
Canst read a fate there, prosperous and clear?
Only the mists, only the weeping clouds:
      Dimness, and airy shrouds.

Beneath, what angels are at work? What powers
Prepare the secret of the fatal hours?
See! the mists tremble, and the clouds are stirred:
      When comes the calling word?

The clouds are breaking from the crystal ball,
Breaking and clearing: and I look to fall.
When the cold winds and airs of portent sweep,
      My spirit may have sleep.

O rich and sounding voices of the air!
Interpreters and prophets of despair:
Priests of a fearful sacrament! I come,
      To make with you my home.

Lionel Johnson

The Joyce's Repentance

I am a sinful man of men,
 Sin's iron pen my feet have trod,
 No single inch in me is whole
 So long my soul hath fought with God.

Just when I think my soul to win,
 I sin some sin, or lie some lie,
 As ducks will leave the clearest springs
 To daub their wings in pools half dry.

The fight with Death is hard and long;
 (Though Death is strong his pace is slow),
 Like helpless ships we turn and toss
 And drift across the waves of woe.

Upon this hinge hangs all my dole,
 My pain of soul, my bitter smart,
 That I have warred with Him who brought
 Me out of naught—rebellious heart!

Once was I good, I once was pure,
 Whilst yet the lure of sin lay hid;
 But as I, ripening, slowly grew,
 I lusted too for things forbid.

Gluttony, sloth, distemper, greed,
    Led me with speed the deathly way,
    Envy and anger, lust and strife
    Made of my life their hideous prey.

O man, my warning take to thee,
    That health shall flee, that youth shall part,
    That as I am, thou yet shalt be,
    But ne'er again as now thou art.

I too was strong, I lived in peace
    Until my lease of strength went by;
    A faggot, now, of wearied bones,
    Upon the stones of death I lie.

Douglas Hyde
(From the Irish)

CCVIII
From

The Ballad of Reading Gaol

There is no chapel on the day
    On which they hang a man:
The Chaplain's heart is far too sick,

Or his face is far too wan,
Or there is that written in his eyes
  Which none should look upon.

So they kept us close till nigh on noon,
  And then they rang the bell,
And the Warders with their jingling keys
  Opened each listening cell,
And down the iron stair we tramped,
  Each from his separate Hell.

Out into God's sweet air we went,
  But not in wonted way,
For this man's face was white with fear,
  And that man's face was grey,
And I never saw sad men who looked
  So wistfully at the day.

I never saw sad men who looked
  With such a wistful eye
Upon that little tent of blue
  We prisoners called the sky,
And at every careless cloud that passed
  In happy freedom by.

The Warders strutted up and down,
  And kept their herd of brutes,
Their uniforms were spick and span,

And they wore their Sunday suits,
But we knew the work they had been at,
By the quicklime on their boots.

For where a grave had opened wide,
There was no grave at all:
Only a stretch of mud and sand
By the hideous prison-wall,
And a little heap of burning lime,
That the man should have his pall,

For he has a pall, this wretched man,
Such as few men can claim:
Deep down below a prison-yard,
Naked for greater shame,
He lies, with fetters on each foot,
Wrapt in a sheet of flame!

And all the while the burning lime
Eats flesh and bone away,
It eats the brittle bone by night,
And the soft flesh by day,
It eats the flesh and bone by turns
But it eats the heart alway.

For three long years they will not sow
Or root or seedling there:
For three long years the unblessed spot

Will sterile be and bare,
And look upon the wondering sky
  With unreproachful stare.

They think a murderer's heart would taint
  Each simple seed they sow.
It is not true! God's kindly earth
  Is kindlier than men know,
And the red rose would but blow more red,
  The white rose whiter blow.

Out of his mouth a red, red rose!
  Out of his heart a white!
For who can say by what strange way
  Christ brings His will to light,
Since the barren staff the pilgrim bore
  Bloomed in the great Pope's sight?

But neither milk-white rose nor red
  May bloom in prison air;
The shard, the pebble, and the flint,
  Are what they give us there:
For flowers have been known to heal
  A common man's despair.

So never will wine-red rose or white,
  Petal by petal, fall
On that stretch of mud and sand that lies
  By the hideous prison wall,
To tell the men who tramp the yard
  That God's Son died for all.

Oscar Wilde

Though Riders Be Thrown

Though riders be thrown in black disgrace,
  Yet I mount for the race of my life with pride,
May I keep to the track, may I fall not back,
  And judge me, O Christ, as I ride my ride.

Douglas Hyde
(From the Irish)

No Coward Soul

No coward soul is mine,
No trembler in the world's storm-troubled sphere:
  I see Heaven's glories shine,
And faith shines equal, arming me from fear.

O God within my breast,
Almighty, ever-present Deity!
        Life—that in me has rest,
As I—undying Life—have power in thee!

        Vain are the thousand creeds
That move men's hearts: unutterably vain;
        Worthless as withered weeds,
Or idlest froth amid the boundless main,

        To waken doubt in one
Holding so fast by thine infinity;
        So surely anchored on
The steadfast rock of immortality.

        With wide-embracing love
Thy spirit animates eternal years,
        Pervades and broods above,
Changes, sustains, dissolves, creates, and rears.

        Though earth and man were gone,
And suns and universes ceased to be,
        And Thou were left alone,
Every existence would exist in Thee.

There is no room for Death,
Nor atom that his might could render void:
    Thou—THOU art Being and Breath,
And what THOU art may never be destroyed.

Emily Brontë

The Winds

"Who are the winds? Who are the winds?"
    —The storm was blowing wild—
"Who are the winds? Who are the winds?"
    —So question'd me the wild-eyed child.
"They are the souls, O child," I said,
    "Of men who long since ceased to hope;
And lastly, wishing to be dead,
    They lay down on the mountain-slope,
    And sighed their wills away;
And nature taking them hath made
    Round and about the world to stray.
Yet oft is waked the fitful pain,
    Which causes them to blow,
And still the passion stirs again

Which vex'd them long ago;
  And then no longer linger they,
  But with a wild shriek sweep away,
  And the green waves whiten to the moon,
  And ships are wreck'd, and shores are strewn."

John Eglinton

The Blue Hills

The Hills, the Blue Hills, what say the Blue Hills?
Old are they—oh!—they are old,
and the stars look down from their Towers of Gold
as the times by the Clock of God are told
unto the Watchman on the wall,
white-robed, vigilant and tall;
and the Sower is breaking with iron drills
the ground, ere he hideth the Seed in the clay,
the Seed of a Flower that will not unfold
till the Hours of the Earth have been rolled away.
The Hills, the Blue Hills—what do they say?
And the Child will pass through the plain and
    will go
to a land that no child shall ever know
a land that's sour, that's cold, that's grey

337

The Harvester will reap, will mow.
Upward and downward the field he will go,
   upward and downward, to and fro,
   upward and downward the long bright day.
   The Hills, the blue, high, lonely shores,
   and who shall name their Grinding Mills?
   Black oat and round the cellar fills,
   and who shall mark their swinging doors?
   Along the fitful lights will play
   till Even cometh up the way—
   to sweep the Chaff from the Threshing Floors.
   The Wild Grey Goose goes croaking by,
   the Swallow passeth from the sky;
   to his Winged Teams that homeward hie,
   a Mystic Waggoner will cry.
   The Hills, the Blue Hills—what do they say?

Philip Francis Little

CCXIII

The Great Breath

Its edges foamed with amethyst and rose,
Withers once more the old blue flower of day:
There where the ether like a diamond glows
   Its petals fade away.

A shadowy tumult stirs the dusky air;
Sparkle the delicate dews, the distant snows;
The great deep thrills, for through it everywhere
    The breath of Beauty blows.

I saw how all the trembling ages past,
Moulded to her by deep and deeper breath,
Neared to the hour when Beauty breathes her last
    And knows herself in death.

A. E.

CCXIV
A Night Piece on Death

By the blue taper's trembling light
No more I waste the wakeful night,
Intent with endless view to pore
The schoolmen and the sages o'er:
Their books from wisdom widely stray,
Or point at best the longest way:
I'll seek a readier path, and go
Where wisdom's surely taught below.

How deep yon azure dyes the sky!

Where orbs of gold unnumbered lie,
  While through their ranks, in silver pride,
The nether crescent seems to glide.
The slumb'ring breeze forgets to breathe,
The lake is smooth and clear beneath,
Where once again the spangled show
Descends to meet our eyes below,
The grounds which on the right aspire,
In dimness from the view retire:
The left presents a place of graves,
Whose wall the silent water laves.
That steeple guides thy doubtful sight
Among the livid gleams of night;
There pass with melancholy state,
By all the solemn heaps of Fate,
And think, as softly-sad you tread
Above the venerable dead,
"Time was, like thee they life possess'd,
"And time shall be, that thou shalt rest."

Those graves, with bending osier bound,
That nameless heave the crumbling ground,
Quick to the glancing thought disclose
Where Toil and Poverty repose.

The flat smooth stones that bear a name,
The chisel's slender help to fame,

(Which ere our set of friends decay
Their frequent steps may wear away.)
A middle race of mortals own,
Men, half ambitious, all unknown.

The marble tombs that rise on high,
Whose dead in vaulted arches lie,
Whose pillars swell with sculptur'd stones,
Arms, angels, epitaphs and bones,
These (all the poor remains of state)
Adorn the rich, or praise the great;
Who while on earth in fame they live,
Are senseless of the fame they give.

Ha! while I gaze, pale Cynthia fades,
The bursting earth unveils the shades!
All slow, and wan, and wrapp'd with shrouds,
They rise in visionary crowds,
And all with sober accent cry,
"Think, mortal, what it is to die."

Now from yon black and fun'ral yew,
That bathes the charnel house with dew,
Methinks I hear a voice begin;
(Ye Ravens, cease your croaking din,
Ye tolling Clocks, no time resound
O'er the long lake and midnight ground)

It sends a peal of hollow groans,
Thus speaking from among the bones.

"When men my scythe and darts supply,
How great a King of Fears am I!
They view me like the last of things:
They make, and then they dread, my stings.
Fools! if you less provok'd your fears,
No more my spectre-form appears.
Death's but a path that must be trod,
If man would ever pass to God:
A port of calms, a state of ease
From the rough rage of swelling seas."

Why then thy flowing sable stoles,
Deep pendent cypress, mourning poles,
Loose scarfs to fall athwart thy weeds,
Long palls, drawn hearses, cover'd steeds,
And plumes of black, that as they tread,
Nod o'er the 'scutcheons of the dead?

Nor can the parted body know,
Nor wants the soul, these forms of woe.
As men who long in prison dwell,
With lamps that glimmer round the cell,
Whene'er their suffering years are run,
  Spring forth to greet the glitt'ring sun:

Such joy, though far transcending sense,
Have pious souls at parting hence.
On earth, and in the body placed,
A few, and evil years, they waste:
But when their chains are cast aside,
See the glad scene unfolding wide,
Clap the glad wing and tow'r away,
And mingle with the blaze of day.

Thomas Parnell

CCXV
Siren Chorus

Troop home to silent grots and caves,
   Troop home! and mimic as you go
The mournful winding of the waves
   Which to their dark abysses flow.

At this sweet hour all things beside
   In amorous pairs to covert creep,
The swans that brush the evening tide
   Homeward in snowy couples keep.

In his green den the murmuring seal
   Close by his sleek companion lies,
While singly we to bedward steal,
   And close in fruitless sleep our eyes.

In bowers of love men take their rest,
   In loveless bowers we sigh alone,
With bosom-friends are others blest,
   But we have none! but we have none!

                      George Darley

CCXVI

Lux in Tenebris

At night what things will stalk abroad,
   What veilèd shapes, and eyes of dread!
With phantoms in a lonely road
   And visions of the dead.

The kindly room when day is here,
   At night takes ghostly terrors on;
And every shadow hath its fear,
   And every wind its moan.

Lord Jesus, Day-star of the world,
  Rise Thou, and bid this dark depart,
And all the east, a rose uncurled,
  Grow golden at the heart!

Lord, in the watches of the night,
  Keep Thou my soul! a trembling thing
As any moth that in daylight
  Will spread a rainbow wing.

Katharine Tynan

CCXVII

O King of the Friday

O King of the Friday
  Whose limbs were stretched on the cross,
O Lord Who didst suffer
  The bruises, the wounds, the loss.

We stretch ourselves
  Beneath the shield of Thy might,
May some fruit from the tree of Thy passion
  Fall on us this night!

Douglas Hyde
(From the Irish)

Mater Dei

She looked to east, she looked to west,
  Her eyes, unfathomable, mild,
That saw both worlds, came home to rest,—
  Home to her own sweet child.
God's golden head was at her breast.

What need to look o'er land and sea?
  What could the winged ships bring to her?
What gold or gems of price might be,
  Ivory or miniver,
Since God Himself lay on her knee?

What could th' intense blue heaven keep
  To draw her eyes and thoughts so high?
All heaven was where her Boy did leap,
  Where her foot quietly
Went rocking the dear God asleep.

The angel folk fared up and down
  A Jacob's Ladder hung between
Her quiet chamber and God's Town.
  She saw unawed, serene;
Since God Himself played by her gown.

Katharine Tynan

The Descent of the Child

Who can bring back the magic of that story,
  The singing seraphim, the kneeling kings,
The starry path by which the Child of Glory
  'Mid breathless watchers and through myriad
    wings
Came, with the heaven behind Him slowly waning,
  Dark with His loss, unto the brightening earth,
The young, ennobled star, that He, so deigning,
  Chose for the heavenly city of His birth?
What but the heart of youth can hold the story,
  The young child's heart, so gentle and so wild,
It can recall the magic of that Glory .
  That dreamed Itself into a little child.

Susan L. Mitchell

Lambs

He sleeps as a lamb sleeps,
　Beside his mother.
Somewhere in yon blue deeps
　His tender brother
Sleeps like a lamb and leaps.

He feeds as a lamb might,
　Beside his mother.
Somewhere in fields of light
　A lamb, his brother,
Feeds, and is clothed in white.

Katharine Tynan

Sheep and Lambs

All in the April evening,
　April airs were abroad;
The sheep with their little lambs
　Passed me by on the road.

The sheep with their little lambs
    Passed me by on the road;
All in the April evening
    I thought on the Lamb of God.

The lambs were weary, and crying
    With a weak, human cry.
I thought on the Lamb of God
    Going meekly to die.

Up in the blue, blue mountains
    Dewy pastures are sweet;
Rest for the little bodies,
    Rest for the little feet.

But for the Lamb of God
    Up on the hilltop green
Only a cross of shame
    Two stark crosses between.

All in the April evening,
    April airs were abroad;
I saw the sheep with their lambs,
    And thought on the Lamb of God.

Katharine Tynan

There is a Green Hill Far Away

There is a green hill far away,
  Without a city wall,
Where the dear Lord was crucified,
  Who died to save us all.

We may not know, we cannot tell
  What pains He had to bear,
But we believe it was for us
  He hung and suffered there.

He died that we might be forgiven,
  He died to make us good,
That we might go at last to heaven,
  Saved by His precious blood.

There was no other good enough
  To pay the price of sin,
He only could unlock the gate
  Of heaven, and let us in.

Frances Alexander

The Crucifixion

At the cry of the first bird
They began to crucify Thee, O cheek like a swan,
It were not right ever to cease lamenting—
It was like the parting of day from night.

Ah! though sore and suffering
Put upon the body of Mary's Son—
Sorer to Him was the grief
That was upon her for His sake.

Kuno Meyer
(From the Irish)

His are the Thousand Sparkling Rills

His are the thousand sparkling rills
    That from a thousand fountains burst,
And fill with music all the hills;
    And yet He saith, "I thirst."

All fiery pangs on battle-fields,
    On fever beds where sick men toss,

Are in that human cry He yields
   To anguish on the cross.

But more than pains that racked Him then
   Was the deep longing thirst Divine
That thirsted for the souls of men:
   Dear Lord! and one was mine.

O Love most patient, give me grace;
   Make all my soul athirst for Thee;
That parched dry Lip, that fading Face,
   That Thirst were all for me.

Frances Alexander

CCXXV

My Christ Ever Faithful

My Christ ever faithful
With glory of angels
And stars in Thy raiment,
Child of the white-footed
Deathless inviolate
Bright-bodied maiden.

Robin Flower
(*From the Irish*)

352

Te Martyrum Candidatus

Ah, see the fair chivalry come, the companions of
    Christ!
White Horsemen, who ride on white horses, the
    Knights of God!
They, for their Lord and their Lover who sacrificed
All, save the sweetness of treading, where He first
    trod!

These, through the darkness of death, the
    dominion of night,
Swept, and they woke in white places at morning
    tide:
They saw with their eyes, and sang for joy of the
    sight,
They saw with their eyes the Eyes of the Crucified.

Now, whithersoever He goeth, with Him they go:
White Horsemen, who ride on white horses, oh,
    fair to see!
They ride, where the Rivers of Paradise flash and
    flow,
White Horsemen, with Christ their Captain: for
    ever He!

Lionel Johnson

The Burial of King Cormac

"Crom Cruach and his sub-gods twelve,"
  Said Cormac, "are but carven treene;
The axe that made them, haft or helve,
  Had worthier of our worship been.

"But He who made the tree to grow,
  And hid in earth the iron-stone,
And made the man with mind to know
  The axe's use, is God alone."

Anon to priests of Crom was brought—
  Where, girded in their service dread,
They minister'd on red Moy Slaught—
  Word of the words King Cormac said.

They loosed their curse against the king;
  They cursed him in his flesh and bones;
And daily in their mystic ring
  They turn'd the maledictive stones,

Till, where at meat the monarch sate,
  Amid the revel and the wine,
He choked upon the food he ate,
  At Sletty, southward of the Boyne.

High vaunted then the priestly throng,
  And far and wide they noised abroad
With trump and loud liturgic song
  The praise of their avenging God.

But ere the voice was wholly spent
  That priest and prince should still obey,
To awed attendants o'er him bent
  Great Cormac gather'd breath to say,—

"Spread not the beds of Brugh for me
  When restless death-bed's use is done:
But bury me at Rossnaree
  And face me to the rising sun.

"For all the kings who lie in Brugh
  Put trust in gods of wood and stone;
And 'twas at Ross that first I knew
  One, Unseen, who is God alone.

"His glory lightens from the east;
  His message soon shall reach our shore;
And idol-god, and cursing priest
  Shall plague us from Moy Slaught no more."

Dead Cormac on his bier they laid:—
  "He reign'd a king for forty years,

And shame it were," his captains said,
  "He lay not with his royal peers.

"His grandsire, Hundred-Battle, sleeps
  Serene in Brugh: and, all around,
Dead kings in stone sepulchral keeps
  Protect the sacred burial ground.

"What though a dying man should rave
  Of changes o'er the eastern sea?
In Brugh of Boyne shall be his grave,
  And not in noteless Rossnaree."

Then northward forth they bore the bier,
  And down from Sletty side they drew,
With horsemen and with charioteer,
  To cross the fords of Boyne to Brugh.

There came a breath of finer air
  That touched the Boyne with ruffling wings,
It stirr'd him in his sedgy lair
  And in his mossy moorland springs.

And as the burial train came down
  With dirge and savage dolorous shows,
Across their pathway, broad and brown
  The deep, full-hearted river rose;

From bank to bank through all his fords,
    'Neath blackening squalls he swell'd and boil'd;
And thrice the wondering gentile lords
    Essay'd to cross, and thrice recoil'd.

Then forth stepp'd grey-hair'd warriors four:
    They said, "Through angrier floods than these,
On link'd shields once our king we bore
    From Dread-Spear and the hosts of Deece.

"And long as loyal will holds good,
    And limbs respond with helpful thews,
Nor flood, nor fiend within the flood,
    Shall bar him of his burial dues."

With slanted necks they stoop'd to lift;
    They heaved him up to neck and chin:
And, pair and pair, with footsteps swift,
    Lock'd arm and shoulder, bore him in.

'Twas brave to see them leave the shore;
    To mark the deep'ning surges rise,
And fall subdued in foam before
    The tension of their striding thighs.

'Twas brave, when now a spear-cast out,
  Breast-high the battling surges ran;
For weight was great, and limbs were stout,
  And loyal man put trust in man.

But ere they reach'd the middle deep,
  Nor steadying weight of clay they bore,
Nor strain of sinewy limbs could keep
  Their feet beneath the swerving four.

And now they slide, and now they swim,
  And now, amid the blackening squall,
Grey locks afloat, with clutching grim,
  They plunge around the floating pall.

While, as a youth with practised spear
  Through justling crowds bears off the ring,
Boyne from their shoulders caught the bier
  And proudly bore away the king.

At morning, on the grassy marge
  Of Rossnaree, the corpse was found,
And shepherds at their early charge
  Entomb'd it in the peaceful ground.

A tranquil spot: a hopeful sound
  Comes from the ever youthful stream,
And still on daisied mead and mound
  The dawn delays with tenderer beam.

Round Cormac Spring renews her buds:
  In march perpetual by her side,
Down come the earth-fresh April floods,
  And up the sea-fresh salmon glide;

And life and time rejoicing run
  From age to age their wonted way;
But still he waits the risen Sun,
  For still 'tis only dawning Day.

Sir Samuel Ferguson

In Tuaim Inbhir

In Tuaim Inbhir here I find
No great house such as mortals build,
A hermitage that fits my mind
With sun and moon and starlight filled.

'Twas Gobban shaped it cunningly,
This is a tale that lacks not proof,
And my heart's darling in the sky
Christ was the thatcher of its roof.

Over my house rain never falls,
There comes no terror of the spear;
It is a garden without walls
And everlasting light shines here.

Robin Flower
(From the Irish)

O Brooding Spirit

O brooding Spirit of Wisdom and of Love,
Whose mighty wings even now o'ershadow me,
Absorb me in thine own immensity,
And raise me far my finite self above!
Purge vanity away, and the weak care
That name or fame of me may widely spread:
And the deep wish keep burning in their stead,
Thy blissful influence afar to bear,
Or see it borne! Let no desire of ease,
No lack of courage, faith, or love, delay
Mine own steps on that high thought-paven way,
In which my soul her dear commission sees:
Yet with an equal joy let me behold
Thy chariot o'er that way by others rolled!

Sir W. R. Hamilton

Desire

With Thee a moment! Then what dreams have
    play!
Traditions of eternal toil arise,
Search for the high, austere and lonely way
The Spirit moves in through eternities.
Ah, in the soul what memories arise!

And with what yearning inexpressible,
Rising from long forgetfulness I turn
To Thee, invisible, unrumoured, still:
White for Thy whiteness all desires burn.
Ah, with what longing once again I turn!

A. E.

Immortality

Age cannot reach me where the veils of God
       Have shut me in,
For me the myriad births of stars and suns
       Do but begin,

And here how fragrantly there blows to me
    The holy breath,
Sweet from the flowers and stars and hearts of
    men,
    From life and death.

We are not old, O heart, we are not old,
    The breath that blows
The soul aflame is still a wandering wind
    That comes and goes;
And the stirred heart with sudden raptured life
    A moment glows.

A moment here—a bulrush's brown head
    In the grey rain,
A moment there—a child drowned and a heart
    Quickened with pain;
The name of Death, the blue deep heaven, the
    scent
    Of the salt sea,
The spicy grass, the honey robbed
    From the wild bee.

Awhile we walk the world on its wide roads
    And narrow ways,
And they pass by, the countless shadowy groups
    Of nights and days;

We know them not, O happy heart,
    For you and I
Watch where within a slow dawn lightens up
    Another sky.

Susan L. Mitchell

When I was Young

When I was young, I said to Sorrow,
    "Come, and I will play with thee":—
    He is near me now all day;
    And at night returns to say,
"I will come again to-morrow,
    I will come and stay with thee."

Through the woods we walk together;
    His soft footsteps rustle nigh me;
    To shield an unregarded head,
    He hath built a winter shed;
And all night in rainy weather,
    I hear his gentle breathings by me.

Aubrey de Vere

363

Renunciants

Seems not our breathing light?
  Sound not our voices free?
Bid to Life's festal bright
  No gladder guests there be.

Ah, stranger, lay aside
  Cold prudence! I divine
The secret you would hide,
  And you conjecture mine.

You too have temperate eyes,
  Have put your heart to school,
Are proved. I recognise
  A brother of the rule.

I knew it by your lip,
  A something when you smiled,
Which meant "close scholarship,
  A master of the guild."

Well, and how good is life,
  Good to be born, have breath,
The calms good and the strife,
  Good life, and perfect death.

Come, for the dancers wheel,
   Join we the pleasant din,
Comrade, it serves to feel
   The sackcloth next the skin.

           Edward Dowden

CCXXXIV
A Little While

A little while, a little while,
   The weary task is put away,
And I can sing and I can smile,
   Alike, while I have holiday.

Where wilt thou go, my harassed heart—
   What thought, what scene invites thee now?
What spot, or near or far apart,
   Has rest for thee, my weary brow?

There is a spot, 'mid barren hills,
   Where winter howls, and driving rain;
But, if the dreary tempest chills,
   There is a light that warms again.

The house is old, the trees are bare,
   Moonless above bends twilight's dome;

But what on earth is half so dear—
    So longed for—as the hearth of home?

The mute bird sitting on the stone,
    The dank moss dripping from the wall,
The thorn-trees gaunt, the walks o'ergrown,
    I love them—how I love them all!

Still, as I mused, the naked room,
    The alien firelight died away;
And from the midst of cheerless gloom,
    I passed to bright, unclouded day.

A little and a lone green lane
    That opened on a common wide;
A distant, dreamy, dim blue chain
    Of mountains circling every side.

A heaven so clear, an earth so calm,
    So sweet, so soft, so hushed an air;
And, deepening still the dream-like charm,
    Wild moor-sheep feeding everywhere.

That was the scene, I knew it well;
    I knew the turfy pathway's sweep,
That, winding o'er each billowy swell,
    Marked out the tracks of wandering sheep.

Could I have lingered but an hour,
　　It well had paid a week of toil;
But Truth has banished Fancy's power;
　　Restraint and heavy task recoil.

Even as I stood with raptured eye,
　　Absorbed in bliss so deep and dear,
My hour of rest had fleeted by,
　　And back came labour, bondage, care.

Emily Brontë

The Comforters

When I crept over the hill, broken with tears.
　　When I crouched down on the grass, dumb in
　　　despair.
I heard the soft croon of the wind bend to my ears,
　　I felt the light kiss of the wind touching my hair.

When I stood lone on the height my sorrow did
　　　speak,
　　As I went down the hill, I cried and I cried,
The soft little hands of the rain stroking my cheek,
　　The kind little feet of the rain ran by my side.

When I went to thy grave, broken with tears,
  When I crouched down in the grass, dumb in
      despair,
I heard the sweet croon of the wind soft in my ears,
  I felt the kind lips of the wind touching my hair.

When I stood by thy cross, sorrow did speak.
  When I went down the long hill, I cried and I
      cried.
The soft little hands of the rain stroked my pale
      cheek,
  The kind little feet of the rain ran by my side.

Dora Sigerson Shorter

Has Sorrow Thy Young Days Shaded?

Has sorrow thy young days shaded,
  As clouds o'er the morning fleet?
Too fast have those young days faded,
  That, even in sorrow, were sweet?
Does Time with his cold wing wither
  Each feeling that once was dear?—
Then, child of misfortune, come hither,
  I'll weep with thee, tear for tear.

Has Hope, like the bird in the story,
  That flitted from tree to tree
With the talisman's glittering glory—
  Has Hope been that bird to thee?
On branch after branch alighting,
  The gem did she still display,
And, when nearest and most inviting,
  Then waft the fair gem away?

If thus the young hours have fleeted,
  When sorrow itself looked bright;
If thus the fair hope hath cheated,
  That led thee along so light;
If thus the cold world now wither
  Each feeling that once was dear:—
Come, child of misfortune, come hither,
  I'll weep with thee, tear for tear.

Thomas Moore

Oft, In the Stilly Night

Oft, in the stilly night,
   Ere Slumber's chain has bound me,
Fond Memory brings the light
   Of other days around me;
     The smiles, the tears
     Of boyhood's years,
   The words of love then spoken;
     The eyes that shone,
     Now dimm'd and gone,
   The cheerful hearts now broken!
Thus, in the stilly night,
   Ere Slumber's chain has bound me,
Sad Memory brings the light
   Of other days around me.
When I remember all
   The friends, so link'd together,
I've seen around me fall
   Like leaves in wintry weather;
     I feel like one
     Who treads alone
   Some banquet-hall deserted,
     Whose lights are fled,
     Whose garlands dead,

And all but he departed!
Thus, in the stilly night,
   Ere Slumber's chain has bound me,
Sad Memory brings the light
   Of other days around me.

Thomas Moore

Who Art Thou, Starry Ghost?

Who art thou, starry ghost,
   That ridest on the air
At the head of all the host,
   And art so burning-eyed
   For all thy strengthlessness?
      World, I am no less
   Than She whom thou hast awaited;
      She, who remade a Poland out of nothingness
      And hath created
Ireland, out of a breath of pride
   In the reed-bed of despair.

Herbert Trench

Gone in the Wind

Solomon! where is thy throne? It is gone in the wind.
Babylon! where is thy might? It is gone in the wind.
Like the swift shadows of Noon, like the dreams
    of the Blind,
Vanish the glories and pomps of the earth in the
    wind.

Man! canst thou build upon aught in the pride of
    thy mind?
Wisdom will teach thee that nothing can tarry
    behind;
Though there be thousand bright actions
    embalmed and enshrined,
Myriads and millions of brighter are snow in the
    wind.

Solomon! where is thy throne? It is gone in the
    wind.
Babylon! where is thy might? It is gone in the wind.
All that the genius of Man hath achieved or
    designed
Waits but its hour to be dealt with as dust by the
    wind.

Pity, thou, reader! the madness of poor
    Humankind,
Raving of Knowledge,—and Satan so busy to
    blind!
Raving of Glory,—like me,—for the garlands I bind
(Garlands of song) are but gathered, and—strewn
    in the wind!

James Clarence Mangan

CCXL

O'Bruidar

I will sing no more songs: the pride of my country
    I sang
  Through forty long years of good rhyme,
    without any avail;
And no one cared even as much as the half of a
    hang
  For the song or the singer, so here is an end to
    the tale.

If a person should think I complain and have not
    got the cause,
  Let him bring his eyes here and take a good
    look at my hand,

Let him say if a goose-quill has calloused this
  poor pair of paws
  Or the spade that I grip on and dig with out
  there in the land?

When the great ones were safe and renowned and
  were rooted and tough,
  Though my mind went to them and took joy in
  the fortune of those,
And pride in their pride and their fame, they gave
  little enough,
  Not as much as two boots for my feet, or an old
  suit of clothes.

I ask of the Craftsman that fashioned the fly and
  the bird,
  Of the Champion whose passion will lift me
  from death in a time,
Of the Spirit that melts icy hearts with the wind of
  a word,
  That my people be worthy, and get, better
  singing than mine.

I had hoped to live decent, when Ireland was quit
  of her care,
  As a bailiff or steward perhaps in a house of
  degree,

But my end of the tale is, old brogues and old
  britches to wear,
  So I'll sing no more songs for the men that care
  nothing for me.

                                        James Stephens
                                (From the Irish of O'Bruidar)

Siberia

In Siberia's wastes
      The Ice-wind's breath
Woundeth like the toothèd steel;
Lost Siberia doth reveal
      Only blight and death.

Blight and death alone.
      No summer shines.
Night is interblent with Day.
In Siberia's wastes alway
      The blood blackens, the heart pines.

In Siberia's wastes
      No tears are shed,
For they freeze within the brain.

Naught is felt but dullest pain,
        Pain acute, yet dead;

Pain as in a dream,
        When years go by
Funeral-paced, yet fugitive,
When man lives, and doth not live,
        Doth not live—nor die.

In Siberia's wastes
        Are sands and rocks.
Nothing blooms of green and soft,
But the snow-peaks rise aloft
        And the gaunt ice-blocks.

And the exile there
        Is one with those;
They are part, and he is part,
For the sands are in his heart,
        And the killing snows.

Therefore, in those wastes
        None curse the Czar.
Each man's tongue is cloven by
The North Blast that heweth nigh
        With sharp scymitar.

And such doom each drees,
 Till, hunger-gnawn,
And cold-slain, he at length sinks there,
Yet scarce more a corpse than ere
 His last breath was drawn.

     James Clarence Mangan

I Saw from the Beach

I saw from the beach, when the morning was
 shining,
 A bark o'er the waters move gloriously on;
I came when the sun from that beach was
  declining,
 The bark was still there, but the waters were
  gone.

And such is the fate of our life's early promise,
 So passing the spring-tide of joy we have known;
Each wave, that we danc'd on at morning, ebbs
  from us,
 And leaves us, at eve, on the bleak shore alone.

Ne'er tell me of glories, serenely adorning
  The close of our day, the calm eve of our night;—
Give me back, give me back the wild freshness of
    Morning,
  Her clouds and her tears are worth Evening's
    best light.

Thomas Moore

Hy-Brasail—The Isle of the Blest

On the ocean that hollows the rocks where ye
    dwell,
A shadowy land has appeared, as they tell;
Men thought it a region of sunshine and rest,
And they called it Hy-Brasail, the isle of the blest.
From year unto year on the ocean's blue rim,
The beautiful spectre showed lovely and dim;
The golden clouds curtained the deep where it lay,
And it looked like an Eden, away, far away!

A peasant who heard of the wonderful tale,
In the breeze of the Orient loosened his sail;
From Ara, the holy, he turned to the west,
For though Ara was holy, Hy-Brasail was blest.

He heard not the voices that called from the shore—
He heard not the rising wind's menacing roar;
Home, kindred, and safety he left on that day,
And he sped to Hy-Brasail, away, far away!

Morn rose on the deep, and that shadowy isle,
O'er the faint rim of distance, reflected its smile;
Noon burned on the wave, and that shadowy
　　shore
Seemed lovelily distant and faint as before;
Lone evening came down on the wanderer's track,
And to Ara again he looked timidly back;
Oh, far on the verge of the ocean it lay,
Yet the isle of the blest was away, far away!

Rash dreamer, return. O, ye winds of the main,
Bear him back to his own peaceful Ara again.
Rash fool! for a vision of fanciful bliss,
To barter thy calm life of labour and peace.
The warning of reason was spoken in vain;
He never revisited Ara again!
Night fell on the deep, amidst tempest and spray,
And he died on the waters, away, far away!

Gerald Griffin

Inscription for a Fountain

Proud of the war, all glorious went the son:
Loathing the war, all mournful went the mother.
Each had the same wage when the day was done:
Tell me, was either braver than the other?

They lay in mire, who went so comely ever:
Here, when you wash, let thought of them abide.
They knew the parching thirst of wound and fever:
Here, when you drink, remember them who died.

Stephen Gwynn

To A Dead Infant

This morn it was she died, the little maid,
a babe of six months old, only six months
in this wide, wide and weary world, and for some
    years
the name shall live upon a marble stone,
and when the name, with its befitting verse,
outgrow the might of marble to retain 't
'twill vanish and be gone out of the world—

for ever. Ah! happy, happy soul returning
in the hour appointed all men to arise,
how know thine own small body when restored
by the great Architect? How wilt thou know?
So short a time, such a long severance—ha!
So little common 'twixt that soul and body!
How find your way back to reclaim that body?
What know you o' the world to recognise
one landmark on the road? Never read a book,
nor learned the great names o' the world, the high,
tremendous titles of its Emperors,
the marching of their armies, launching forth
o' their fleets upon the Deep, the state intrigues,
the plots, the counterplots, th' ambitions foiled,
pleasures indulged, the pastimes, pains, the labours.
Unknown and never learned—not even forgotten!
As primitive, as unsophistical
as maiden dead in howling Thrace long ago,
child of some roving tribe, and suckled on
the wild mare's milk, or widening its round eyne
on uncouth herdsmen clothed in skins, who had
    blown
on pipes, in grassy places lone, unfenced—
except by mountain ranges, where their sires
had cried to countless flocks a thousand years,

uninterrupted in vast Phrygia,
whose offspring, apprehending nothing, went
unsighing whither thou are gone, to where
an Everlasting Lamp shines constantly.
Earth to the earth—away! Sweet seraph—lo!—
as does the sea exceed the moisture one
may hold i' the hand's hollow, so your knowledge
to-night exceeds the lore of all the world.
(An infant dead knows more than all the world!)
And as, for purpose of repose, we must
let down the weary arm to the side at last,
the moisture trickling to the ground, erstwhile
reposing in the hollow hand, not so
need you for evermore relax, but hold
fast in your heart, which is the soul's right hand,
the lucid Vision of Eternity.
Dear soul, sweet saint, how do I reverence thee!
This morn, it was, she died; in one short hour,
just six months old, an infant. Lo! let the name
straightway be graved upon a snow-white Tomb,
a blanchèd, carven image spreading wide
its noon-white wings and clasping to its breast
one single gleaming ear of wheat—uptending
to Heaven—shall be the Infant's Monument.

Philip Francis Little

Weary

Some grave is known to God,
Some green sequestered sod,
Wrapped in whose fragrant fold
I shall no more grow cold.

And God hath saints who sing,
And holy hands which bring
Offerings and gifts more meet
Than mine, who clasp His feet

And ask to toil no more,
But, on the golden shore,
To rest, and dream, and be
As God's dead men are, free.

Yet, since He frees me not,
I wait and wonder what
Undreamed-of thing God hath
Better to give than death.

George A. Chadwick

The Last Music

Calmly, breathe calmly all your music, maids!
Breathe a calm music over my dead queen.
All your lives long, you have nor heard, nor seen,
Fairer than she, whose hair in sombre braids
    With beauty overshades
      Her brow, broad and serene.

Surely she hath lain so an hundred years:
Peace is upon her, old as the world's heart.
Breathe gently, Music! Music done, depart:
And leave me in her presence to my tears,
    With music in mine ears:
      For sorrow hath its art.

Music, more music, sad and slow! she lies
Dead: and more beautiful than early morn.
Discrowned am I, and of her looks forlorn:
Alone vain memories immortalize
    The way of her soft eyes,
      Her musical voice low-borne.

The balm of gracious death now laps her round,
As once life gave her grace beyond her peers.
Strange! that I loved this lady of the spheres,

To sleep by her at last in common ground:
　　When kindly sleep hath bound
　　Mine eyes and sealed mine ears.

Maidens! make a low music: merely make
Silence a melody, no more. This day,
She travels down a pale and lonely way:
Now, for a gentle comfort, let her take
　　Such music, for her sake,
　　As mourning love can pay.

Holy my queen lies in the arms of death:
Music moves over her still face, and I
Lean breathing love over her. She will lie
In earth thus calmly, under the wind's breath,
　　The twilight wind, that saith:
　　Rest! worthy found, to die.

Lionel Johnson

Non Dolet

Our friends go with us as we go
Down the long path where Beauty wends,
Where all we love forgathers, so
Why should we fear to join our friends?

Who would survive them to outlast
His children; to outwear his fame—
Left when the Triumph has gone past—
To win from Age not Time a name?

Then do not shudder at the knife
That Death's indifferent hand drives home;
But with the Strivers leave the Strife,
Nor, after Caesar, skulk in Rome.

Oliver Gogarty

O Blest Unfabled Incense Tree

O blest unfabled Incense Tree,
That burns in glorious Araby,
With red scent chalicing the air,
Till earth-life grow Elysian there!

Half buried to her flaming breast
In this bright tree, she makes her nest,
Hundred-sunned Phoenix! when she must
Crumble at length to hoary dust!

Her gorgeous death-bed! her rich pyre
Burnt up with aromatic fire!

Her urn, sight-high from spoiler men!
Her birthplace when self-born again!

The mountainless green wilds among,
Here ends she her unechoing song!
With amber tears and odorous sighs
Mourned by the desert where she dies!

George Darley

What is Worth the Singing?

Since Youth has all too brief a stay,
And Joy, alas, is never sure,
For Love but holds a balance bringing
His ache together with his ease;
If such fair things, though they may sway
Life to the deeps, may not endure,
And life has given our hearts to these—
What, then, is left us worth the singing?

Years pass; but one thing will remain
Unmoved amid our fevered breath,
Unvexed amid the vexed hours flinging
Spent foam upon the weed-strewn shore;
Which thing alone can bring again

What Time has rendered naught. Lo, Death
Is Love and Joy and Youth—and more.
That, then, is left us worth the singing.

Cecil French

The Three Poplars

I shall have three grey poplar trees above me when
  I sleep;
the poplars will not sway or swing, nor like the
  willow weep,
but upright as the staff of one who watcheth o'er
  his sheep.

Some fount may open silvern lips near by; not far
  away
the harvester his voice may lift in solemn joy;
  three grey
great poplars will refresh him with their shade in
  the noonday.

And when to every creature Night repose and
  respite brings,
profound my sleep, the while to me the dew-wet
  meadow clings,

soft garment of the Poor, which is the cerecloth,
    too, of Kings.

As when the Shadow Hand of Eventide the toiling
    Bee
at last will homeward guide, and guide unto her
    sheltering tree
the weary singing Bird, so may the kind night
    come for me!

I shall have three grey poplar trees above me when
    I sleep;
the poplars will not sway or swing, nor like the
    willow weep,
but upright as the staff of one who watcheth o'er
    his sheep.

Philip Francis Little

CCLII

When

When mine hour is come
Let no teardrop fall
And no darkness hover
Round me where I lie.

389

Let the vastness call
One who was its lover,
Let me breathe the sky.

Where the lordly light
Walks along the world,
And its silent tread
Leaves the grasses bright,
Leaves the flowers uncurled,
Let me to the dead
Breathe a gay goodnight.

A. E.

CCLIII

That

. . . alone
From all eternity.

What is that beyond thy life,
And beyond all life around,
Which, when thy quick brain is still,
Nods to thee from the stars?
Lo, it says, thou hast found
Me, the lonely, lonely one.

Charles Weekes

The Indian Upon God

I passed along the water's edge below the humid
 trees,
My spirit rocked in evening light, the rushes
 round my knees,
My spirit rocked in sleep and sighs; and saw the
 moorfowl pace
All dripping on a grassy slope, and saw them
 cease to chase
Each other round in circles, and heard the eldest
 speak:
*Who holds the world between His bill and made us
 strong or weak*
Is an undying moorfowl, and He lives beyond the sky.
The rains are from His dripping wing, the moonbeams
 from His eye.
I passed a little farther on and heard a lotus talk:
Who made the world and ruleth it, He hangeth on a
 stalk,
For I am in His image made, and all this tinkling tide
Is but a sliding drop of rain between His petals wide.
A little way within the gloom a roebuck raised his
 eyes

Brimful of starlight, and he said: *The Stamper of*
   the Skies,
He is a gentle roebuck; for how else, I pray, could He
Conceive a thing so sad and soft, a gentle thing like me?
I passed a little farther on and heard a peacock say:
Who made the grass and made the worms and made
   my feathers gay,
He is a monstrous peacock, and He waveth all the night
His languid tail above us, lit with myriad spots of light.

                                            W. B. Yeats

                        CCLV

                    Immortality

We must pass like smoke or live within the spirit's
   fire;
For we can no more than smoke unto the flame
   return
If our thought has changed to dream, our will
   unto desire,
   As smoke we vanish though the fire may burn.

Lights of infinite pity star the grey dusk of our
   days:
Surely here is soul: with it we have eternal breath:

                        392

In the fire of love we live, or pass by many ways,
   By unnumbered ways of dream to death.

                                        A. E.

Four Ducks on a Pond

Four ducks on a pond,
A grass-bank beyond,
A blue sky of spring,
White clouds on the wing;
What a little thing
To remember for years—
To remember with tears!

                William Allingham

The Outcast

Sometimes when alone
At the dark close of day,
Men meet an outlawed majesty
And hurry away.

They come to the lighted house;
They talk to their dear;
They crucify the mystery
With words of good cheer.

When love and life are over,
And flight's at an end,
On the outcast majesty
They lean as a friend.

A. E.

I Lie Down With God

I lie down with God, and may God lie down
    with me;
The right hand of God under my head,
The two hands of Mary round about me,
The cross of the nine white angels
From the back of my head
To the sole of my feet.
May I not lie with evil,
And may evil not lie with me.

Eleanor Hull
(*From the Irish*)

Finis

Finis to all the manuscripts I've penned
And to life's fitful fever here "The End."
"The End" to limewhite women golden-tressed
And in Christ's hands at Judgment be the rest!

Robin Flower
(From the Irish)

Note

The Memory of the Dead

(Page 178)

I have been requested to publish the following note on "The Memory of the Dead":—

"The poem entitled 'The Memory of the Dead' was published in the *Nation* newspaper in April 1843, when I was in my twentieth year . . . Some persons have believed, or affected to believe, that I am ashamed of having written it, and would gladly, if I could, disown its authorship. Those who know me do not need to be told that this idea is without foundation. I think the Irish race should be grateful to men who, in evil times, however mistaken may have been their policy, gave their lives for their country. But I have no sympathy with those who preach sedition in our own day, when all the circumstances are radically altered. In my opinion no real popular interest can now be furthered by violence.

JOHN K. INGRAM.

"Dublin, 1900."

Index of Authors and Titles of Poems

* See also translations from the Gaelic.

401

* See also translations from the Gaelic.

* See also translations from the Gaelic.

⋆ See also translations from the Gaelic.

---

* See also translations from the Gaelic.

** See also translations from the Gaelic.

410

Translations From the Gaelic

Index of First Lines

417

422

423